A Handbook for Inclusion Man

Are you responsible for inclusion in your school?

As an Inclusion Manager, you have a strategic role that covers a great deal more than special educational needs, and requires a specific knowledge and skill set in order to steer your school towards inclusion. *A Handbook for Inclusion Managers* presents a wide range of information, providing plenty of fresh ideas and a stimulus for reflection on your practice.

This comprehensive and accessible text examines recent legislation, including the Common Assessment Framework, and provides information on how to gain accreditation for your work on inclusion. It will help you to create and manage an inclusive school, covering a wide range of knowledge and skills including:

- getting the best from your staff;
- how to interpret data to judge the achievement of different groups in your school;
- where the money for inclusion comes from;
- what inclusive teaching and learning look like;
- working with special schools;
- community cohesion;
- reporting to governors, parents and Ofsted;
- working on an inclusion strategy.

Providing a framework that can be adapted to suit individual schools, *A Handbook for Inclusion Managers* includes a checklist of good practice to enable you to keep track of your school's progress. The author provides numerous references to useful organisations, websites and publications to make your life easier.

This invaluable companion for Inclusion Managers, SENCOs and anyone working on inclusion gathers together the background information and practical advice you need to successfully manage a truly inclusive learning environment.

Ann Sydney is an educational consultant and school inspector with a background in special educational needs.

WITHDRAWN

nasen
Helping Everyone Achieve

Other titles published in association with the National Association for Special Educational Needs (nasen):

Living with Dyslexia, Second Edition: The Social and Emotional Consequences of Specific Learning Difficulties/Disabilities
Barbara Riddick
978–0–415–47758–1 (PB)

Dyspraxia 5–14: Identifying and Supporting Young People with Movement Difficulties
Christine Macintyre
978–0–415–54397–2 (HB)
978–0–415–54396–5 (PB)

Teaching Foundation Mathematics: A Guide for Teachers of Older Students with Learning Disabilities
Nadia Naggar-Smith
978–0–415–45164–2

Language for Learning: A Practical Guide for Supporting Pupils with Language and Communication Difficulties across the Curriculum
Sue Hayden
978–1–84312–468–9

The Rob Long Omnibus Edition of Better Behaviour
Rob Long
978–1–84312–470–2

The Special School's Handbook
Michael Farrell
978–0–415–41685–6 (HB)
978–0–415–41686–3 (PB)

The SEN Handbook for Trainee Teachers, NQTs and Teaching Assistants
Wendy Spooner
978–1–84312–404–7

The New nasen A–Z of Reading Resources
Suzanne Baker and Lorraine Petersen
978–1–84312–441–2

Beating Bureaucracy in Special Educational Needs
Jean Gross
978–0–415–44114–8

P Levels in Mainstream Settings: Meeting the Needs of All Pupils
Lorraine Petersen and Ann Fergusson (forthcoming)
978–0–415–43791–2

Diversity and Personalised Learning
John Visser (forthcoming)
978–0–415–46752–0

A Handbook for Inclusion Managers

Steering your school towards inclusion

Ann Sydney

Routledge
Taylor & Francis Group

LONDON AND NEW YORK

nasen
Helping Everyone Achieve

First published 2010
by Routledge
2 Park Square, Milton Park, Abingdon, Oxon OX14 4RN

Simultaneously published in the USA and Canada
by Routledge
270 Madison Avenue, New York, NY 10016

Routledge is an imprint of the Taylor & Francis Group, an informa business

© 2010 Ann Sydney

Typeset in Garamond 3 by
Florence Production Ltd, Stoodleigh, Devon
Printed and bound in Great Britain by
CPI Antony Rowe, Chippenham, Wiltshire

British Library Cataloguing in Publication Data
A catalogue record for this book is available from the British Library

Library of Congress Cataloging in Publication Data
Sydney, Ann.
  A handbook for inclusion managers: steering your school towards
  inclusion/Ann Sydney.
      p. cm.
   Includes index.
  1. Inclusive education – Great Britain.   2. Mainstreaming in education –
  Great Britain.   3. Education and state – Great Britain.   I. Title.
  LC1203.G7S94 2010
  371.9'0460941 – dc22   2009011025

ISBN 10: 0–415–49197–5 (hbk)
ISBN 10: 0–415–49198–3 (pbk)

ISBN 13: 978–0–415–49197–6 (hbk)
ISBN 13: 978–0–415–49198–3 (pbk)

nasen is a professional membership association, which supports all those who work with or care for children and young people with special and additional educational needs. Members include teachers, teaching assistants, support workers, other educationalists, students and parents.

nasen supports its members through policy documents, journals, its magazine *Special!*, publications, professional development courses, regional networks and newsletters. Its website contains more current information such as responses to government consultations. **nasen**'s published documents are held in very high regard both in the UK and internationally.

Contents

Illustrations

Figures

Tables

Acknowledgements

I'd like to thank all the pupils and colleagues I have worked with over many years. I have learned a lot from all of them. Since 1996 I have had the privilege of watching many fantastic teachers in their classrooms, some accomplishing minor miracles in trying circumstances. For help and encouragement with this book, my thanks go to Bob Black, Dr Michael Farrell, Geoff Hancock, Anne Rafferty, Keith Swain, Rob Thomas and Selwyn Ward. Particular thanks for their generosity go to:

- Rosemary Leeke, headteacher of South Camden Community School;
- Vicki Paterson, executive head of Brindishe and Hither Green primary schools.

Thanks also to Jon Sydney, Katherine Sydney and Christeen Skinner, for reminding me that there's life beyond the laptop.

The author's payments for this book have been donated to the Nava Kiran orphanage for street children near Kathmandu, where 'inclusion' has a very basic meaning. To make a donation, go to the website at www.friendsofconservation.org.uk/donateform. asp?link=exodus, and click on Himalaya Social and Education Fund.

Permissions

I would like to thank:

- Dr Michael Farrell for permission to use an excerpt on assessing pupils with learning difficulties from *The Special Education Handbook*, 4th ed., London: Routledge, 2009, p. 225;
- Rosemary Leeke for permission to use the South Camden Community School's inclusion policy and access plan;
- Vicki Paterson for permission to use Brindishe primary school's inclusion policy.

Ofsted documents reproduced with kind permission from the Office of Public Sector Information, under the terms of the Click-Use Licence.

Web addresses: These are correct at April 2009.

Abbreviations

(Beware, your local authority may have its own names and acronyms.)

ADHD	attention deficit and hyperactivity disorder
AEN	additional educational needs
ASD	autistic spectrum disorder
ASDAN	Award Scheme Development and Accreditation Network
AQA	Assessment and Qualifications Alliance
BESD	behavioural, emotional and social difficulty
BEST	Behaviour and Educational Support Team
CAF	Common Assessment Framework
CGS	care, guidance and support
COPE	Certificate of Personal Effectiveness
CRE	Commission for Racial Equality
CSIE	Centre for Studies on Inclusive Education
CVA	contextual value added
DCSF	Department for Children, Schools and Families
DDA	Disability Discrimination Act
DfES	Department for Education and Skills (now DCSF)
EAL	English as an additional language
EMA	Educational Maintenance Allowance
EMAG	Ethnic Minority Achievement Grant
EP	educational psychologist
EWO	Educational Welfare Officer/Attendance Officer
EYFS	Early Years Foundation Stage
FFT	Fischer Family Trust
FSM	free school meals
G&T	gifted and talented
HLTA	Higher Level Teaching Assistant
HMI	Her Majesty's Inspectorate of Education
ICT	information and communication technology
IEP	Individual Education Plan
IQM	Inclusion Quality Mark
LA	local authority
LAC	looked-after children (children in care)
LDD	learning difficulties and disabilities

LEA	local education authority
LSA	learning support assistant
NFER	National Foundation for Educational Research
PD	physical disability
PDWB	personal development and well-being
PLASC	Pupil Level Annual School Census
PMLD	profound and multiple learning difficulties
PRU	Pupil Referral Unit
PSHCE	personal, social, health and citizenship education
PSP	Pastoral Support Plan
RAISE/RAISEonline	Reporting and Analysis for Improvement through School Self-Evaluation
SEF	Ofsted School Self-Evaluation Form
SEN	special educational needs
SENCO	Special Educational Needs Co-ordinator
SENDA	Special Educational Needs and Disability Act
SLD	severe learning difficulty
SSEN	statemented pupils with special educational needs
TA	teaching assistant
VI	visually impaired

Introduction

This handbook is aimed at mainstream school managers who have strategic responsibility for inclusion. You may be called an Inclusion Manager or do the job by a different name. The job title 'Inclusion Manager' means many different things in different schools. It's certainly more than being a Special Educational Needs Co-ordinator (SENCO) and arguably more than being a Head of Learning Support. In some schools, you will have responsibility for the whole range of 'soft' management – the pastoral side, pupils with additional difficulties and disabilities, looked-after children (LAC), travellers and those with English as an additional language (EAL) – not to mention laptops, the personalised curriculum, staff training and meeting every visiting professional. In other schools, you may delegate part of this role to a Special Educational Needs Co-ordinator or a pastoral manager.

Yours is a strategic role rather than a day-to-day management or teaching position. An Inclusion Manager needs to be able to analyse, plan and evaluate provision, looking at the whole child in the context of the Every Child Matters programme that followed the Children Act in 2004. Whatever you are called, you would normally be a member of the senior management team because of your whole-school responsibilities. You will be managing change and need to have the clout to do this. Being on the leadership team also sends out a message that inclusion is important and central to your school.

Managing inclusion cuts across every aspect of the school, but the methods you employ are the same in each situation: collect data and review, plan, implement, monitor and evaluate. The priorities in the school improvement plan should drive all your work, but you will have an important part to play in setting those priorities.

In writing this handbook, I have been selective: there is so much going on in the field, and the field boundaries seem to be constantly extending and changing. This handbook covers the legal framework that underpins inclusion. It ranges across the different aspects of your role and offers criteria that you can evaluate your school's performance by. Where it doesn't cover the background in detail, it refers you to websites and other sources that fill this in for you. Although it is Anglocentric in terms of the law, many of the ideas and suggestions apply to schools in other parts of the UK education system and beyond. I hope it is written in clear, down-to-earth language. Legislation and websites change and expand, and of course you will want to add your own examples of good practice.

Chapter 1

The big picture

Who is included?

That might seem a silly question, but the answer is it varies across the country, with an average of about 1 per cent of pupils in special schools. 'Inclusion' has been a burning issue for many years. Historically, some groups of children and young people were denied education because of their learning and physical difficulties. This was followed by separate specialist schooling for pupils with different special educational needs (SEN), then a move towards educating everyone in mainstream schools. Seen as the opposite of 'exclusion', inclusion would appear to be something that everyone would want, like peace and freedom, but there is a strong argument that some pupils achieve better in specialist provision, or in a flexible mix of special and part-time mainstream schooling. One argument against inclusion is that it conflicts with maximising test and exam results because pupils with additional needs tend to perform below the national average. They can also make extra demands on time and staffing, not least when pupils have behavioural difficulties. Recently the emphasis has widened from including special educational needs to more general 'social cohesion'. Inclusion is about including everyone and offering them the best opportunities in life. It has more to do with the Every Child Matters agenda – every child should be safe and healthy, enjoy and achieve at school, make a contribution to the community and be prepared for their future economic well-being – than about location. To simplify writing this handbook, I have assumed that you are in a mainstream school where pupils with a wide range of needs are included.

'Evaluating Educational Inclusion' (Ofsted 2000) says that inclusion applies to:

- boys and girls;
- minority ethnic and faith groups, travellers, asylum seekers and refugees;
- pupils learning English as an additional language;
- pupils with special educational needs;
- pupils at risk of disaffection or exclusion;
- gifted and talented (G&T);
- looked-after children;
- sick children;
- young carers;
- children from families under stress;
- pregnant schoolgirls and young mothers.

Collectively, some or all of these groups are known as 'SEN', 'LDD', 'SSEN', 'vulnerable children', or additional educational needs (AEN). The terms are often loosely used and are sometimes used inter-changeably, but there is some agreement on the following definitions.

- **SEN**: Pupils with special educational needs have a learning difficulty that hinders access to the curriculum. Their needs would fall into one of the four categories:
  - cognitive and learning;
  - physical and sensory (including medical needs);
  - social, emotional and behavioural;
  - communication and interaction.
- **LDD**: Pupils with learning difficulties and disabilities are those identified and provided for at School Action, School Action Plus on your SEN register, or who have a statement of educational need. LDD and SEN are often used interchangeably.
- **SSEN**: Pupils with statements of special educational need.
- **Vulnerable children**: Looked-after children/children in care, plus pupils with learning difficulties and disabilities, plus other children whose lives beyond school put them at risk of underachievement.
- **AEN**: Additional educational needs usually describes vulnerable pupils plus gifted and talented, refugees and asylum seekers, and those learning English as an additional language.

What inclusion is not

Inclusion is not about cherry-picking. Having a child on your roll with a minor physical disability while excluding pupils with behavioural, emotional and social difficulties (BESD) is not inclusion. Telling parents in the prospectus that you are unable to accommodate wheelchair users because some of your rooms are inaccessible is not inclusion either.

There is a lot of legislation to get your head around, but it is fundamental. At times you may need to refer to the original Acts and guidance, but in the remainder of this chapter, I have summarised significant current (2008) legislation.

Admissions

The Special Educational Needs Code of Practice 2001 says:

> All schools should admit pupils with already identified special educational needs, as well as identifying and providing for pupils not previously identified as having SEN. Admission authorities may not refuse to admit a child because they feel unable to cater for their special educational needs. Pupils with special educational needs but without statements must be treated as fairly as all other applicants for admission. Admission authorities must consider applications from parents of children who have special educational needs but no statement on the basis of the school's published admissions criteria. Such children should be considered as part of the normal admissions

procedures. Admission authorities cannot refuse to admit children on the grounds that they do not have a statement of special educational needs or are currently being assessed.

At the same time, it says that 'A parent's wish to have their child with a statement educated in the mainstream should only be refused in the small minority of cases where the child's inclusion would be incompatible with the efficient education of other children.' The last phrase in particular is one that has exercised lawyers.

Before pupils transfer to your school, it is helpful if you can get information on whether they have been on their previous school's SEN register at any level, and, if so, what their needs and provision were. Which strategies worked? This may involve staff visiting feeder schools, if that is manageable. Preparation needs to start well before the new intake arrives – ideally as soon as the local authority has finalised the admissions list – so that you can start allocating to classes and planning provision, staffing and possibly equipment. Most local authorities consult schools before naming them on a child's statement, though they can direct the school to take statemented pupils. Admissions for pupils with statements are usually decided in advance of those of other pupils.

What do you provide for vulnerable new pupils at transition? Most schools have a person identified for transitions whose job is to visit feeder schools and collect pupil information and also to make any special provision for induction day. Some offer the opportunity for pupils and a teaching assistant (TA) to visit the receiving school together, or for the primary teaching assistant to spend some of the first week of the new term in the receiving school, supporting the pupil and passing on tips to staff. Most schools provide a 'buddy' pupil or extra adult support in the shape of a teaching assistant in class, or access to a learning mentor. Don't underestimate the threat of change for some pupils, especially those on the autistic spectrum.

Reluctance to admit a pupil with special needs usually occurs when schools consider that they already have a high proportion of pupils with SEN, feel they could not cope with a particular profile of needs, or determine that they have inadequate financial resources for meeting the needs of the pupil. Casual/mid-phase admissions cause a particular problem because support and provision really need to be there from the start.

Exclusions

Pupils with statements of special need are almost four times more likely to be excluded from school than the rest of the school population despite such exclusion being condemned as bad practice. Pupils with attention deficit and hyperactivity disorder (ADHD) and those on the autistic spectrum are the most commonly excluded (National Foundation for Educational Research 2005: 3). There are strict rules for the total length of exclusions in any one year and the reasons pupils can be excluded. Where provision is unsuitable, it should be possible to bring forward a statemented pupil's annual review and resolve the problems by providing alternatives within the school. Alternatively, a move to other provision can be managed. In France, Belgium, the Netherlands, Denmark and Germany, schools are not allowed to exclude pupils; the head must find them another placement.

Regrettably, some schools assess certain needs as too complex for them and opt for exclusion as a means of bringing the situation to the local authority's attention. Delegating resources to schools is expected to increase schools' capacity to cater for pupils' special educational needs. As Inclusion Manager, you need to ensure that resources are deployed so that staff have the skills to handle difficult pupils and a continuum of provision is there to fall back on.

A school must refer to Department for Children, Schools and Families (DCSF) guidance in adopting and reviewing its exclusions policy. Its policy on behaviour can vary from DCSF guidance, but there 'must be a good and properly justified reason to depart from it'. The guidance can be found at www.teachernet.gov.uk/wholeschool/behaviour/exclusion/guidance.

When a pupil is excluded, he or she has to be offered full-time education elsewhere within six days. The excluding school can help this transition by forwarding not just information about the offences or behaviour that led to the exclusion but clear data about the pupil's academic achievement and standards, together with a description of what has been covered in the curriculum and samples of work. Staff in Pupil Referral Units not surprisingly find it difficult to prepare lessons that match pupils' ability when they have a steady stream of excluded, difficult or vulnerable pupils coming through the door with no useful background information. Once a pupil is excluded, the local authority has to carry out the Common Assessment Framework (CAF) for the pupil, if it has not been done already. Pupils stay on the excluding school's roll until the appeal deadline passes or until an appeal is heard.

There are now fewer incidents of 'unofficial' exclusions than there were in the past, though this category still includes pupils with statements. Government departmental guidance in 2008 made it clear that unofficial exclusion has no legal basis and should not be proposed by teachers or agreed to by parents. After all, exclusion on its own is unlikely to be an effective strategy for improving pupils' behaviour, especially if it is due to an inability to behave appropriately. You should ask yourself what the school is hoping to gain from the exclusion, and whether you could get the same result through action that doesn't have the same long-term effect on the individual pupil. Does your behaviour policy encourage and reward positive behaviour? You should be clear, before the situation escalates towards exclusion, whether the behaviour might be due to a special educational need that has not been recognised. You may need to involve the educational psychologist (EP). Pupils on the autistic spectrum will benefit least from exclusion because of their inability to cope with change.

Successful reintegration after a period of exclusion will depend on the motivation of the pupil, parental cooperation, detailed planning (probably by you) for re-entry, support and monitoring. If there isn't a special educational need and the behaviour stems from disaffection or lack of interest in school – and you will only find this out from the pupil – what changes to the curriculum can be made without compromising the provision for other pupils?

Sometimes the context of your school is not right for a particular pupil. For example, a pupil with ADHD might not be coping well in a very large school. Rather than exclusion, a 'managed move' can give the pupil a fresh start if there is support in place at the receiving end from day one. Ideally, receiving staff will have been informed about the pupil's triggers and difficulties, and they will have had time to consider classroom arrangements, friendship groups, support, the curriculum and modifications to lesson planning. Managed moves work best when you have built up relationships with senior management in other local schools and are totally honest with each other. Other schools may have expertise in working with particular needs. It helps if you have a neutral person – for example, a member of the Behaviour and Educational Support Team (BEST) – acting as a go-between and initially supporting the pupil. You could agree to a trial period, with a settling-in review after a month and a review of the placement after a term. You could do the same for that school next time.

The Children Act and Every Child Matters

The Children Act 2004 has meant the reorganisation of local provision under the umbrella of Children's Services, and it brought in five key outcomes for children, the same across all services. These outcomes, with a nod towards Maslow's hierarchy of needs, are also the basis for Ofsted inspections under the heading of 'Every Child Matters'. Every child should:

- Be healthy.
- Stay safe.
- Enjoy and achieve.
- Make a positive contribution to the community.
- Achieve economic well-being/be prepared for the next stage of life.

The whole idea is that services are built around children and families, and that all children have opportunities and safeguards. Money has been channelled through the Children's Fund, local authorities, and voluntary and community groups to set up a whole range of projects designed to improve child health inequalities, improve attendance and help families out of poverty. It is concentrated on children up to age 13 and will continue until 2011.

Special educational needs and disability

The SEN Code of Practice says that children with special educational needs should have their needs met. They should have a broad, balanced and relevant curriculum. This should normally be in a mainstream school. The children's views should be taken into account, and parents have an important role as partners in their child's education. The code also sets strict time limits within which the statementing process should be completed. From the time that the parent is informed that an assessment will be done, the local authority has ten weeks for everyone concerned to submit their evidence, unless this coincides with the summer holidays. In many local authorities, statements are becoming increasingly rare. In 2007, about 2 per cent of pupils nationally had a statement of educational need, and this included all the pupils in special schools.

The Disability Discrimination Act (DDA) says that it is unlawful for a responsible body (school governing body or local education authority (LEA)) to discriminate against a disabled child. Discrimination takes the form of less favourable treatment because of a disability, or failure to make reasonable adjustments in relation to education and associated services. It is unlawful to discriminate in the provision of education and associated services as well as in admissions and exclusions. The Act covers physical access, access to the curriculum and the availability of information in several ways. The duty to make reasonable adjustments is limited in relation to pre-16 education; the reasonable adjustment duty does not apply to auxiliary aids and services because this is already covered by the SEN Code of Practice.

The 2008 review of this legislation did make changes to examination dispensation. It said that if a disabled pupil is exempted from part of an examination because no reasonable adjustment can be made for him to be able to take it, then the examination grade can reflect those parts of the examination that he was able to take. The Act also says that 'physical alterations to schools are not required under the reasonable adjustment duty as it is anticipated that these will be achieved through a longer term and more strategic approach to improving access to school buildings through the planning duties'. The duties require local education authorities and non-education-authority schools to prepare an accessibility strategy aimed at increasing the extent to which disabled pupils can participate in the schools' curriculum, improving the physical environment of schools and improving the delivery of information. There is no date by which this should be in place, which makes the legal requirement pretty toothless. Your school should have an accessibility plan, showing how it will improve access over time. Your governors should be aware of the requirement because it is a statutory obligation, and your local authority should have a plan for making schools accessible. A clear example of a school access plan is in the appendix to this book.

The Special Educational Needs and Disability Act (SENDA) 2001 strengthened the right of children with special educational needs to attend a mainstream school unless their parents choose otherwise or it is incompatible with 'efficient education for other children' and there are no 'reasonable steps' that the school and local authority can take to prevent that incompatibility.

In 2006, over 400 cases of complaint against schools and local authorities went to the Special Educational Needs and Disability Tribunal (SENDIST); about half of these were pupils with statements. Many of the complaints were about the lack of provision of extra equipment and aids.

The Disability Discrimination Act of 2005 took equal rights for disabled people further. Schools and other public sector bodies must be proactive and promote equality of opportunity for disabled people and involve disabled people in their planning and policies, whether they are pupils, staff or parents. The Disability Rights Commission in spring 2006 gave comprehensive Guidance on Disability in Schools. You can read this at www.teachernet.gov.uk/wholeschool/disability/disabilityandthedda. By December 2007, all schools – mainstream and special – had to have written their own Equality Scheme, saying how they would promote equality. To promote equality, you must monitor the achievement of disabled pupils as a distinct group. This is not the same as pupils with special educational needs. Pupils with cancer, diabetes, severe asthma or epilepsy may be registered disabled but may not be on your SEN register because they do not meet other criteria you set when you set up the register. Your Disability Equality Scheme should include your priorities until 2010. It should include all school users – staff, parents, governors, and so on. Details can be found at www.dotheduty.org. One of the differences between this and previous legislation is that schools must take steps to take into account people's disabilities, even where that involves more favourable treatment. Exam certificates, for example, no longer show any exam concessions given, such as an amanuensis.

What the National Curriculum says

The National Curriculum states that there are three 'principles for inclusion':

- setting suitable learning challenges;
- responding to diverse learning needs;
- overcoming potential barriers to learning and assessment.

This translates into challenging stereotypical views so that pupils can view difference positively. Methods include:

- using teaching approaches to match different learning styles and incorporate all the senses;
- planning challenging work for all, including those whose ability is beyond their language skills;
- using materials that reflect diversity and promote positive images;
- planning for continuity for those pupils with extended absences;
- using different types of groupings/individual work to meet everyone's learning needs;
- offering boys and girls the same opportunities in the curriculum and ensuring equal access to equipment;
- giving pupils with disabilities or medical needs support, adaptations or aids to access activities so they have the fullest possible participation. This can include using outside agencies;
- planning teaching and assessment to cater for different learning styles;
- challenging all forms of harassment;
- allowing participation in clothing that is appropriate to their religious beliefs – for example, in PE – providing this does not compromise safety;
- planning work that builds on pupils' interests and cultural experiences;
- using the available special arrangements in Standard Attainment Tests and exams for those who need it;
- helping pupils to manage their emotions and behaviour;
- ensuring that all pupils can be included and participate fully and safely in educational visits;
- using accessible texts and giving opportunities in every lesson for talking and understanding the subtleties of the English language.

Gender equality

The attainment of girls starts to outstrip that of boys at nursery, and they are a long way ahead at GCSE, especially in subjects reliant on literacy. Despite this, there is still a wide gap between the earnings of men and women, who now expect to work full time but have the major responsibility for childcare and housework. There is still a need for gender equality legislation.

In the Equality Act 2006, the government introduced new duties for the public sector. Schools must comply with these. You must have by now produced and published a Gender Equality Scheme identifying goals and actions to meet them. You must have consulted with employees and stakeholders in its development, monitored and reviewed progress, and published an annual report on progress with the action plan. Schools must develop and publish an equal-pay policy and gender-impact assessments of all legislation and policy developments. It is a requirement that pupils, staff, trade unions and those using school services should have been involved in the production of the Gender Equality Scheme. You could consult with these groups through questionnaires or focus groups to determine the success of the action plan. Essentially, you have to find out if your school users feel they have equal access to everything that goes on there, such as challenging gender stereotypes in the curriculum with careers advice, or whether fathers feel involved in their children's learning.

Some local authorities have produced a model scheme for schools, and you can find these on the internet. For example, Lambeth local authority's is at www.lambeth.gov.uk/ Services/EducationLearning/SchoolsColleges/ModelGESForSchools.htm.

Race and equality

The 2006 report 'Ethnicity and Education' stated that 21 per cent of the maintained primary school population and 17 per cent of the maintained secondary school population were classified as belonging to a minority ethnic group.

Minority ethnic pupils are more likely to experience deprivation than white British pupils, and their parents are less likely to have gone on to higher education. Most make less progress than white British pupils in primary school, but they make more progress in secondary. However, Gypsy and Roma pupils, travellers of Irish heritage and white and black Caribbean pupils continue to perform below similar white British pupils during secondary school. Within the black African group, there is a wide range of outcomes, 'black Africa' encompassing a huge range of countries. Pupils with English as an additional language now perform as well at GCSE (five grade A*–C) as white British, but not if you count in English GCSE.

Regarding race and equality, there are legal obligations that all schools have in common, whether they are multi-ethnic or not. These include duties under the Race Relations (Amendment) Act 2000 to maintain a written statement of policy on race equality and to be proactive in promoting equality of access and opportunity for all pupils. There are duties under the requirements of the National Curriculum to plan approaches to teaching and learning so that all pupils can take part in lessons fully and effectively, and so that all pupils are prepared for life in a multi-ethnic society. Following on from the Macpherson (Stephen Lawrence) Inquiry, schools have a duty to address and prevent racism in its various forms, and to send regular reports to their local authority about incidents which arise.

The principles behind recent legislation can be summarised as:

- ensuring equality;
- recognising difference;
- promoting cohesion.

In 2006, the Equality Act came into force, which aimed to simplify and rationalise the patchwork of previous acts covering different aspects of equality. It established the Commission for Equality and Human Rights that covers the six strands of equality: age, disability, race, religion and belief, gender and sexual orientation, and human rights.

Schools often deal well with disability, race and gender in their policies but are weak on the other areas, including sexual orientation. Homophobic bullying is a recognised common cause of teenage suicide. Does your school's policy affirm equality for gay pupils and staff? It should be clear that your equality policy applies to the whole school community, not just pupils. There is guidance on how schools should respond to the Equality Act at www.teachernet.gov.uk/_doc/11059/Equality_legislation. This recommends you write a single Equality Plan covering all the plans set out in the guidance. You could cross-reference policies that naturally link together.

- Do your school policies comply with this legislation? Do they reflect your values and beliefs and do they promote inclusion?
- Does everyday practice follow these good intentions? How can you check?
- Are review dates for policies on your school calendar and the governors' calendar?

You are not just working within the framework of national legislation, but also within the guidelines of what your local authority has planned. Each local authority will have an inclusion strategy, and you should be aware of this when you write/review yours. What is in the local authority strategy has implications for curriculum, teaching and learning, school organisation and structures, funding mechanisms and school management. Most local authorities have theirs on their website.

Chapter 2

How well is your school doing?

Compared with the national picture

The Ofsted report 'Special Educational Needs and Disability: Towards inclusive schools' (2004) suggested the following criteria for good progress for pupils with SEN in mainstream schools. I have seen nothing to supercede this:

- At least 80 per cent of pupils make a gain of one level (either National Curriculum or P levels) at KS3.
- At least 34 per cent of pupils below level two in English in year 7 gain one level by the end of KS3, and 55 per cent at level two gain one level by the end of KS3.
- Pupils withdrawn for substantial literacy support make an average of double the normal rate of progress.
- Attendance of pupils with special needs is above 92 per cent and unauthorised absence is low.

You can look at data that compare your school with the national picture by going to www.raiseonline.org/login. You will need a user name and password specific to your school to access it. RAISE stands for Reporting and Analysis for Improvement through School Self-Evaluation. Schools can 'drill down' online through the information to individual pupil level. RAISE only holds validated (checked with schools) data back to 2005 at Key Stages 1–4 for all mainstream maintained schools. Unvalidated data is available annually in the autumn term after SATs and validated data early in the summer term. As well as SATs, the data come from the Pupil Level Annual School Census (PLASC/Form 7) information your school routinely submits in January.

What RAISEonline shows

'Attainment' means how well your pupils score on tests, or what standards they are reaching.

Contextual value added (CVA) means how well your pupils' test scores have improved since their previous SATs compared to similar pupils in similar schools. CVA takes account of not just how well pupils performed on tests but also the level of deprivation they experience, their ethnicity and gender and special educational needs. So it is a good indicator of how much difference the school makes. If the CVA score is 100.00, then that group is making as much progress as the average similar child nationally. Below 100, they are not doing as well. Above 100.00, and you are making a positive difference. In secondary schools, the reference is to 1000.00

If RAISEonline indicates that your school is performing in maths at the fifth percentile, then only 5 per cent of schools nationally are doing better at maths.

These 'snake graphs' below show the improvement of pupils between two key stages. The percentile rank compares their progress to the progress of pupils in similar schools and already accounts for various indicators of deprivation, so you are comparing like with like as far as possible. You can see the pattern over three years. These graphs show a school where the CVA results have been improving rapidly between 2005 and 2007: the school is making an increasing difference to their pupils' life chances.

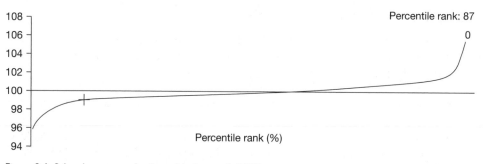

Figure 2.1 School contextual value added overall: **2007**

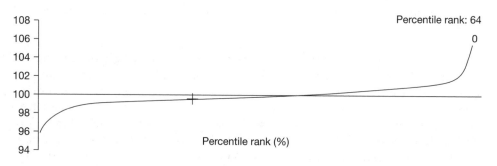

Figure 2.2 School contextual value added overall: **2008**

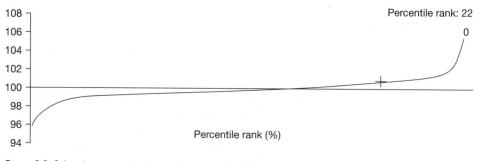

Figure 2.3 School contextual value added overall: **2009**

The 'cross graphs', as in Figure 2.4 below, show CVA scores graphed against attainment. If your cross appears in the top right quarter, as does the school below, you are a school that not only gets good results but your value-added is also above average: you make a difference to pupils. In the school below, the Average Points Score is nearly four above the national average and its CVA score is nearly 102.00, so despite some deprivation/low starting points, the pupils are doing very well. Conversely, if you appear in the bottom left quarter, the situation is 'challenging'.

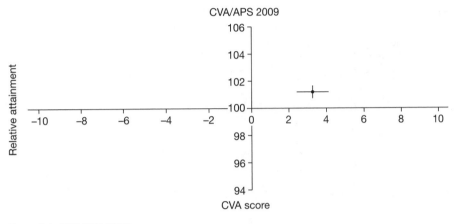

Figure 2.4 CVA/APS 2009

Table 2.1.14 in RAISEonline will show you whether these results are statistically significantly above or below average. Remember that this is describing a situation that has already happened because RAISEonline is always based on last year's results.

The online charts and tables 2.1.15 to 2.1.18 show the value-added scores for different groups in a school. The chart on p.14 (Figure 2.5) shows ethnicity. On it, there are four minority ethnic groups, all small cohorts. Because of the small size of these groups, the vertical line through the small marker square shows the range within which the score might be accurate. Only the white and black Caribbean groups on the graph are necessarily underperforming. Only the Indian pupils are necessarily outperforming the white British group. Be vigilant when interpreting statistics where the cohort size is very small: the picture may not be as clear-cut as you first think.

You can see how well your school performs against the national picture, trends and the performance of different groups in your school – not just girls compared with boys, but different ethnic groups, pupils of different abilities, pupils with English as an additional language, those at School Action, statemented pupils and School Action Plus, travellers, and looked-after children. You can see at a glance if these groups are underachieving, but beware of jumping to conclusions. Again, the sub-groups may be made up of a very small number of pupils so that the performance of one pupil can skew the figures. This is particularly true in the School Action/statemented figure: obviously it depends on what additional difficulty or disability these individuals had. They are

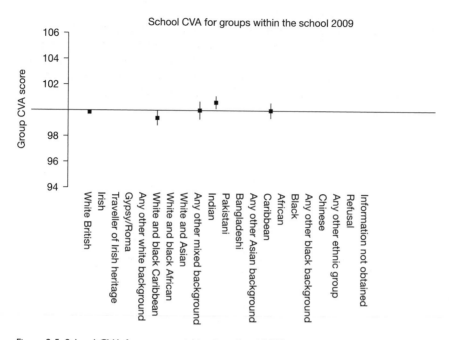

Figure 2.5 School CVA for groups within the school 2009

being compared nationally against a very broad range of need. Comparing the School Action results with the overall school and national results can give an indication of how good the provision in mainstream classes is for pupils with low level (School Action) additional needs. If your School Action figures are lower than the rest of your school and compare badly against national figures, follow up on how well teachers are differentiating in class and how much general in-class support is directed at these pupils.

The scatter graph (usually chart 2.1.19 in RAISEonline) gives you a simple picture of underachievement and picks out boys and girls. It is possible for schools to pick out who the underachievers were by going to the RAISEonline website and interrogating it, rather than relying on the paper report.

RAISEonline will give you information that you can use to contribute to the school's Self-Evaluation Form; for example, it will tell you how well pupils with English as an additional language perform. One of the good things is that it shows contextual value added (CVA) data so that even if your raw test results are low, your pupils may be doing very well compared to their starting points.

What RAISEonline doesn't show

RAISEonline doesn't give a true picture if you have high pupil mobility. Look at where it says 'coverage' – for example, on chart 2.1.19, which shows underachievement of boys and girls. This is the percentage of pupils who have been present at the end of two key stages. Many schools with high mobility produce their own data for the pupils who have been with them continuously and find this useful supplementary material for their self-evaluation. It could be, of course, that your mid-phase entrants are higher achievers, and so the picture might not look so rosy.

RAISEonline holds very little data if you're working in a middle school where you don't have two sets of Standard Attainment Tests results to compare, or indeed for sixth forms. All data are slightly out of date because they refer to the previous year's test results, so remember this when you look at the breakdown of pupils by year, and add a year. Inspectors will have access to RAISEonline before they arrive in your school but will want to verify pupils' current achievement and standards first-hand in class and from the school's assessment data, and so will you.

There is an online tutorial for RAISEonline at www.standards.dfes.gov.uk/esp/.

You can download 'Using data, improving schools' from the Ofsted website. Type in www.ofsted.gov.uk and go to publications. This report explains more than RAISEonline: it goes into Fischer Family Trust (FFT) and other packages, and explains how inspectors use school data.

Data within your school

What baseline data does your school have on pupils? Is the same data collected for mid-phase entries? On transfer from Key Stage 2, many secondary schools are wary of SATs scores and feel they are inflated or are a result of teaching to the test. Do you have any joint moderation with primary schools? A long summer holiday has passed, and new pupils are under considerable stress. Do you need to test all the pupils again immediately? Where pupils arrive with poor literacy, it will be necessary to do reading tests that are diagnostic so that you can base interventions on the needs this test indicates. Who is responsible for this in your school? It would seem logical that the English department are involved, not just Learning Support staff. Many schools use Cognitive Ability Tests as a baseline to supplement the SATs scores, but relatively few have samples of work for staff to see. Perhaps pupils could bring some of their work on induction day? You will normally have good information on statemented pupils, but do you know who is on lower levels of the SEN register in their primary school, what has been tried already and what worked?

What data does your school have on the progress of pupils from different groups? You won't know this unless you have an effective tracking system. Remember, you are collecting data so that you can see patterns and improve the provision of services. You probably analyse test results by subject, year group and gender already, but can you also analyse by ethnic group or disability? Are pupils with behavioural, emotional and social difficulties or looked-after children making as much progress as others? Are gifted and talented pupils underachieving? Without this data, how do you know if your work towards inclusion is effective? Your data manager should be able to pull out these pupils' results for you. You can get data for individual pupils from RAISEonline. Most schools have a simple colour-coded method of seeing if pupils have reached their targets, gone beyond them or are underachieving. Others take it that bit further and show the difference in Average Points Scores from one key stage to the next, or express progress in terms of sub-levels each year. Compare the performance of pupils in your targeted group across different subjects. This will give you a focus for lesson observations to see what is and is not working with these pupils and to share your feedback with teachers. The effectiveness of your tracking will depend on how accessible these data are to teachers. It is going to be more effective if individual teachers hold the data and know how to use them as well as how to input the raw numbers.

There is a link between attainment, additional difficulties and disabilities, behaviour and attendance. Before you can put action in place, you need to know how different groups are attending and why this is so. Does your data system allow you to do this? Office staff should be making first-day calls. Any absence by looked-after children or those on the 'at risk' register should be closely and quickly followed up.

Your school should have a calendar of particular dates through the year when data are collected and analysed so that comparisons can be made over time. The results of this analysis should be shared with staff, governors, pupils and parents. It could be valuable training for your governing body to have one governor sitting in on the analysis.

P scales are for pupils working below National Curriculum level one. They start from a very low baseline at level P1 to level P8. They show minute changes in performance. For example, P1(1) for any subject describes encountering activities and experiences. Pupils may be passive or even resistant, but they are encountering them. They may show simple reflex responses such as startling. Any participation is fully prompted. Level P8 in using and applying mathematics describes pupils talking about, recognising and copying simple repeating patterns and sequences in a variety of settings, and their next step would be National Curriculum level one. More information is at www.qca.org.uk. Assessment will necessarily involve close observation. Where pupils are working at P levels in mainstream, staff with expertise will need to train teaching assistants in observation and recording, as they will have closest and most regular contact. Class teachers will need to be familiar with the scales and have access to other experienced schools for moderation of assessments. With some pupils with severe learning difficulties or profound and multiple learning difficulties, you may find pupils' progress static or regressing as their condition deteriorates. In this situation the goal is to maintain their skills.

Once you have a picture of how well your pupils are doing compared to similar pupils nationally, and compared to their starting points, share this with all school staff. Who, apart from you, should be monitoring the progress of pupils with additional difficulties and disabilities?

Pupils with Individual Education Plans (IEPs) should have reviews at least two times a year, and pupils with statements should also have an annual multi-agency review. IEPs are not a statutory requirement. Many schools have individual planning and recording for all pupils; in this case, IEPs would not be required. IEPs are only useful where they make recommendations that do not apply to the rest of the class. As the move towards personalised learning gets into gear, the need for separate IEPs for a significant minority is less obvious. The National Strategies give examples of how to record interventions as part of class lesson plans and how to record outcomes.

How inclusive is your school already?

Before you can write your school inclusion policy, you need to know what is going on in your school. Then you have to write a strategy/development plan. After that you can write a policy that reflects reality rather than being a wish list.

What is the current reality compared to what your school might aspire to? What are your priorities? You will need a plan to identify who you need to help you, what resources you will need and a target date for each action. Some of these points can be actioned directly by you; many of them can be delegated. Some of them are to do with how well you and your team raise the profile of inclusion and how you manage change. You will have to devise ways of evaluating where you are at the outset. For example, the question 'Do all pupils feel safe?' may need a questionnaire to be completed at home. Anything you write in the 'Evidence' column of the tables below will be useful for completing the school Self-Evaluation Form.

In the following tables, tick against the sentences that describe your school currently. You can photocopy these charts and use them for self-evaluation.

Table 2.1 School inclusion self-assessment: pupils with additional needs

Pupils with additional needs	Evidence
☐ Feel safe	
☐ Develop self-esteem and confidence as independent learners	
☐ Access a wide curriculum that suits their needs	
☐ Make good progress in relation to their starting points, and their achievements are in line with those of pupils with similar difficulties and circumstances	
☐ Attend as well as other pupils (around 92 per cent secondary, 94 per cent primary)	
☐ Have a low and falling rate of exclusion	
☐ Contribute to the school community	

Table 2.2 School inclusion self-assessment: teachers

Teachers	Evidence
☐ Follow the school's Inclusion and related policies	
☐ Have high expectations of all pupils and set challenging targets	
☐ Know enough about pupils and their additional needs to match work to them in every lesson	
☐ Develop and share expertise	
☐ Communicate well with parents, specialist teachers, support staff and external agencies	
☐ Can identify pupils with possible additional needs	

Table 2.3 School inclusion self-assessment: pastoral staff

Pastoral staff	Evidence
❒ Follow the inclusion policy	
❒ Work to retain pupils	
❒ Use information and data about pupils with additional needs to inform their actions	
❒ Communicate with SENCO, Inclusion Manager, specialist teachers, parents and outside agencies	
❒ Provide welcoming and useful induction for new pupils including mid-phase	
❒ Prepare pupils well for the next stage of learning	

Table 2.4 School inclusion self-assessment: teaching assistants and learning mentors

Teaching assistants and learning mentors	Evidence
❒ Take opportunities to improve their skills	
❒ Are familiar with pupils' needs and have expertise in meeting them	
❒ Subscribe to and follow the school's policies	
❒ Communicate well with class teachers, tutors, parents, pupils, SENCO and external agencies	
❒ Are fully involved in the school	

Table 2.5 School inclusion self-assessment: volunteers

Volunteers	Evidence
❒ Are aware of the inclusive ethos of the school and subscribe to relevant policies	
❒ Are CRB (Criminal Records Bureau) checked and are aware of the school's child protection procedures	
❒ Are clear about their role and have relevant training	
❒ Communicate well with their line manager	

From Ann Sydney (2010) *A Handbook for Inclusion Managers*, London: Routledge. © 2010 Ann Sydney

Table 2.6 School inclusion self-assessment: parents

Parents	Evidence
☐ Feel involved in their children's education and confident about approaching staff	
☐ Understand and take part in assessment, decision-making and reviews	
☐ Understand their children's targets and how to help them	

Table 2.7 School inclusion self-assessment: governors

Governors	Evidence
☐ Ensure the school meets its statutory requirements regarding inclusion	
☐ Work to retain pupils	
☐ Have a schedule to regularly review all relevant policies	
☐ Are regularly informed of developments related to inclusion	
☐ Have a nominated governor (or more than one) who takes a particular interest in inclusion issues and visits school	

Table 2.8 School inclusion self-assessment: senior management team

Senior management team	Evidence
☐ Provide and regularly review a curriculum that suits the needs of all learners	
☐ Ensure the inclusion policy is followed	
☐ Rigorously evaluate provision in the light of pupil's progress	
☐ Focus lesson observations on the needs of different groups	
☐ Integrate systems and procedures for SEN with the arrangements for all pupils	
☐ Provide resources and staffing to make inclusion effective	
☐ Share expertise with other schools	
☐ Provide data that allow different groups of pupils, as well as individuals, to be tracked	
☐ Give out the message that this is an inclusive school	

From Ann Sydney (2010) *A Handbook for Inclusion Managers*, London: Routledge. © 2010 Ann Sydney

Table 2.9 School inclusion self-assessment: subject leaders

Subject leaders	Evidence
❒ Monitor teaching and learning in their subject areas to ensure the needs of all pupils are met	
❒ Link with specialist teachers and support staff to ensure the scheme of work in their subject is relevant to different groups in the school and identifies sensitive issues	

Table 2.10 School inclusion self-assessment: admin staff

Admin staff	Evidence
❒ Follow up first-day absences	
❒ Are given child protection refresher training alongside other staff every three years	

Table 2.11 School inclusion self-assessment: outside agencies

Outside agencies	Evidence
❒ Have timely and full information about pupils	
❒ Are informed via the Common Assessment Framework of relevant pupils' needs	
❒ Are involved in assessment, decision making and reviews with parents	
❒ Have a clear means of evaluating progress and clear exit criteria	
❒ Keep the Inclusion Manager informed	

Table 2.12 School inclusion self-assessment: local authority

Local authority	Evidence
❒ Provide a range of relevant training	
❒ Provide a support network for Inclusion Managers	
❒ Provide a continuum of relevant alternative provision	

Chapter 3

Ethos

This is about the 'feel' of your school – how you work together as a community to make pupils and staff feel they belong.

'Special Educational Needs and Disability: Towards inclusive schools' (DfES 2004) set out criteria for self-evaluation. One of these was that 'the pupils make a positive contribution to the school community'. The supporting criteria for this were:

- There is an active approach to personal and social development as well as to learning in the school, especially to lessen the effects of the divergence of social interests between older pupils with SEN and their peers.
- All pupils learn about disability issues.
- Pupils with SEN have a voice that is heard regularly in the school.
- Pupils with SEN are able to participate fully in the life of the school.
- There are well-defined and consistently applied approaches to managing difficult behaviour.

Do pupils want to come to your school?

What is the unauthorised attendance rate at your school? What is the trend? As failing schools 'turn around', it is noticeable that their unauthorised attendance rate gets better as the quality of teaching and learning improves. Truancy, whether it is for specific lessons, whole days or longer, leads to underachievement, and sometimes it is hard to distinguish the cause from the effect. Present policy is to threaten, then prosecute parents, who may not feel they have control of their 15-year-old, or may themselves not value what the school offers. There is not much research on why truants truant, but it could be argued that truancy is a symptom of unmet needs. The simplest link may be between poor literacy and numeracy, but that might be putting the cart before the horse because irregular attendance will make it worse. It certainly doesn't apply to those truants who might choose their lessons and days carefully. Sometimes it can be uncomfortable to think that truancy is a rational response. Truants may need to be heard and to feel that they have a voice in their education. Pupils could be truanting for lots of reasons: not doing homework because it's too hard or there's nowhere at home to do it, falling behind because they've been absent legitimately and there's no chance to catch up, feeling their option choices were ignored, earning money, feeling picked on in class by teachers or pupils, or having to put up with poor teaching week after week. It might be condoned because parents have had similar experiences and want to protect their child. First, you need to find out why individual pupils truant, then put in some measures to overcome the problem, whether this is offering homework clubs with computers available, catch-up classes, a more relevant and engaging curriculum or alerting subject leaders to complaints.

Ofsted defines an educationally inclusive school as 'one in which the teaching and learning, achievements, attitudes and well-being of every young person matters'. It starts at the top. To be blunt, does the headteacher want an inclusive school? Talk to him or her about their philosophy. The head can set the moral framework of the school and the underlying sentiment that guides the beliefs, customs and practices of the school. It is difficult to be 'inclusive' if you are in a local authority that practises selection at eleven years old, but within your school, you can build inclusive practices. What are the benefits? Some of the highest-achieving schools (not always those with the highest exam results) are those where inclusion is a priority. All groups of pupils achieve well because there is an emphasis on matching the curriculum and lessons to different groups. There is a sense of harmony in the school and confidence among pupils because their views and cultures are valued.

Principles of inclusion

There are three underlying principles of inclusion: equality, diversity and cohesion.

Equality

All pupils are of equal value and should have equal opportunities to learn and to be successful. This is enshrined in national legislation, as you saw in the previous chapters. Schools are expected to remove barriers to learning and success.

Diversity

All pupils are of equal value and should be treated equally, but this does not necessarily mean that they should all be treated exactly the same. Significant differences of culture, outlook, narrative and experience should be recognised and respected. For example, it is unjust to treat pupils new to English as if they are already fluent speakers.

Belonging and cohesion

It is important that all pupils feel that they belong – to the school, to the neighbourhood and to Britain. Belonging involves shared stories and symbols, a sense of having a stake in the well-being and future development of the community. It means feeling welcomed and accepted as well as being able and encouraged to take part and contribute. One way you can signal this to new entrants is to show you value the achievements of leavers. Some secondary schools hold 'proms' (even some primary schools do it!) and display photographs around the school to give a sense of graduation or rite of passage. Prize days celebrate academic achievement and more. A banner on the front of the school celebrating exam successes flags this up to the whole community.

The perception of whether your school is inclusive starts out in the community. It isn't all your responsibility, but you should be able to influence those staff who are responsible for community links and publicity. What is the public image of your school? What stories are you getting in the local press? Are there opportunities for local people to come into the school? Some schools run English language classes for parents. Others run how-to-handle-your-teenager's/nursery-child's-behaviour classes, or literacy, numeracy or information technology (IT) classes under the heading 'how to help your child with homework'. Is your website kept up to date and does it look 'inclusive'? That is, are images chosen with care to show the full range of pupils and their achievements? Are the inclusion policy and related policies, such as behaviour and race, on the website? Are frequently asked questions and answers available in community languages? Under the Disability Discrimination Act, your website should be accessible in terms of layout, size and colour of font. There are various quality marks you can apply for: Google 'quality mark for web accessibility' or 'audit web accessibility'.

First impressions

As you enter the school grounds, is the disabled parking bay marked clearly? Could somebody with visual impairment find the entrance easily? Is there an alternative to any steps there might be to the entrance? Are there automatic doors? Is there an induction loop for people with hearing impairments at the reception desk? Is there an adapted toilet close to the entrance? Are reception staff welcoming to all comers? Is there basic information about frequently asked questions in common community languages? What feedback are you asking for from visitors to school and users of the website?

There is quite a lot to question even about the initial welcome to school. It can even include the colour scheme. Visually impaired pupils, staff and visitors will have more independence if there is clear colour contrast around doors, steps and other features of the building. Why not set pupils and parents to audit your school's inclusivity? They may pick up issues that you have stopped noticing because they are so familiar.

While some schools claim to be 'inclusive', visitors can get mixed messages when they find that 'Special Needs' is in the post-war temporary hut across the playground, or at the top of the Victorian triple-decker. If you are going to give the message that inclusion matters in your school, put services for inclusion at the centre of your building, integrated with the rest of the school and totally accessible. This gives a strong message that every child does matter. Your school may have benefited from the School Access Initiative money that was available for modifications from 2002–8. Check if there is any funding now. Consider what you call this part of your school. 'Special Needs department' is too narrow, and 'Learning Support' may not cover all you need it to include. 'Student Services' may cover too much. Whatever you decide fits your role, raise its profile with lively displays, stationery and email signatures that bring it to people's attention.

In some schools the inclusion policy does not reflect that individual school's practice. It should. A policy is not a wish list. All staff, not just teachers, should have had the opportunity to contribute to the inclusion policy or question it during its formulation. Your school should have an inclusion policy which describes your core beliefs, admissions policy, how the curriculum, resources and buildings ensure equality, how staffing is deployed, and what your expectations are. Chapters 9 and 10 cover this in more detail and include examples.

Accessibility

An accessibility plan should show how you are adapting the school to be more welcoming and accessible to the whole range of pupils, parents and staff. If there are currently some stubbornly inaccessible areas – to wheelchair users, for example – your school's plan should say how the school will make modifications to get around this, including perhaps the timetable for doing so. It should also say how the curriculum and teaching methods are adapted to match various needs. See the appendix for an example from South Camden Community School.

Make sure you cover the whole range of 'inclusion'. Describe current provision and how it is evaluated. Explain how often the policy will be reviewed and how you will ensure that it is followed. You should also say how complaints can be made and to whom, and what the process is for taking the matter further. Who is the Named Person in your school (probably you), and what is the name of any governor with an overview of inclusion (i.e., the chair of governors)?

Across the country, staffing does not mirror the diversity of the school population. Your school has a legal obligation to ensure that employment law on discrimination is followed. Do you have the opportunity to ensure that there is a question about attitudes to inclusion in the job interview? Once staff are (Criminal-Records-Bureau checked and) appointed, how are they inducted? What do they need to experience as well as read? Do subject staff know any community languages, have experience teaching English as a second language or experience teaching particular learning difficulties or disabilities?

How are the governors involved? How are they kept informed of your journey towards being an inclusive school? Are they aware of the legal framework? Do you invite them to training days? Do you have a regular slot for inclusion updates at full governors' meetings and at meetings of the committee that looks at these issues?

Including pupils with behavioural difficulties

One of the areas of inclusion that can be controversial in a school is how behaviour is dealt with. This is high on the list of parents' concerns, whether it is their child's difficulty or a classmate's. You will probably have pupils identified as having behavioural, emotional and social difficulties. Some of these may be diagnosed as being on the autistic spectrum or having ADHD, and some of those may be on medication. They will be on your SEN register and may have a statement of special educational need. These in a sense are the straightforward ones because all staff can identify them as having difficulties that are objectively assessed and are seen in some ways as beyond the pupil's control. Much more difficult are the pupils who are troubling rather than troubled, who persistently misbehave or may as yet be undiagnosed. There are still schools that have two different systems working against each other: on one hand, the Learning Support staff works with outside agencies to modify identified behaviourial difficulties; on the other side, a pastoral system moves pupils up through the thresholds of different punishments, then out of the school. How integrated are your systems? How good is the communication between staff? What opportunities are there for pastoral and Learning Support staff to meet with other agencies to discuss cases? How early are parents involved as partners?

Different models of pastoral systems

The traditional model

In primary schools, class teachers work with the SENCO and have a complete view of the child's pastoral and academic needs. Teachers change their class groups each year. Pupils may have home/school books.

In secondary schools, pupils are in tutor groups, keeping the same group and tutor for five years. The tutors' job is to monitor attendance and punctuality and to link with home. They meet their class each morning and again briefly at the start of the afternoon. Tutors may be responsible for delivering personal, social, health and citizenship education under the guidance of a subject leader. They use planners to record merits and detentions. There is a Year Head, who is the next line of management, and there is also a Key Stage Manager. In this model, the pastoral and academic sides of the child are kept fairly separate.

Alternatives

- Vertically grouped tutor groups can work well because younger and more vulnerable pupils can find a 'champion' in older pupils. Where the vertical grouping extends to sixth formers, it is important that they retain some privileges, have access to a sixth-form common room and time for private study. Otherwise they can feel they are getting the short straw.
- Heads of Year stay in the same role, where they gain expertise, rather than move up the school with their Year group. This does, however, mean that relationships are severed.
- Heads of Year 7 and 11 stay in that role, but 8–10 move on with their pupils. Both of these mean that new Year 8's, the year where progress can stall, have less stability and support.

Rebranding Heads of Years

Now that data is readily accessible around the school, many schools have changed so that a Progress Leader takes charge of all aspects of pupil life for their Year group. They communicate with Learning Support and attend multi-agency meetings together with the tutor. There are usually progress meetings several times a year for each pupil to check on underachievement and to set targets.

House systems

Some schools layer a House system on top of this. This is useful where you have a very large school, and gives an institution of manageable size to relate to. It also gives opportunities for competition at Hogwarts.

Vulnerable pupils

Where you have a unit or designated specialist provision with a number of vulnerable pupils, the size of any secondary school can be daunting. There may be problems just moving around the building or feeling safe. An alternative would be to set up smaller classes for teaching the core curriculum, but to mirror this in the pastoral system. A handful of pupils – perhaps a friendship group – share a tutor who may be attached to the Learning Support/Inclusion department.

The Key Stage Manager's role, if one exists, is to ensure the curriculum is suitable, government initiatives are in place, and to have an overview of standards and progress in their key stage.

Personal, social, health and citizenship education (PSHCE) delivery is through a dedicated lesson each week with trained, well-prepared and possibly specialist staff who are assessing pupils' progress. This gives pupils the message that it is worth doing. There is now a one-year training course in PSHCE.

How schools combat racism

If you work in a city school, it is likely you have a very diverse school population, but there are still large areas of the country that are monocultural. It is these schools as much as the inner city schools that need to think about how they model race equality. Research for the Department for Education and Skills (DfES) in 2002 (Research Report RR365) concluded that mainly white schools are frequently not sufficiently aware of racism in the school population and in the local neighbourhood. There is insufficient awareness among staff of principles and good practice for helping pupils to acquire and use English as an additional language. In general, mainly white schools do not adequately prepare their pupils for adult life in a society that is culturally and ethnically diverse. Many teachers in mainly white schools are critical of the poor quality of their initial training with regard to teaching minority ethnic pupils, and are aware that this now needs urgent attention in their continuing professional development.

Five years have passed since the DfES report, but does this still describe your school? If it does, look at your Continuing Professional Development schedule urgently.

The following is a compilation of guidance from a range of local authorities, some of whom have very low numbers of minority ethnic pupils but who have considered how schools best operate in a multi-cultural society. There are implications for staff training, the curriculum, leadership and management. Remember, racist bullying is where the victim perceives it to be racist, whether the onlookers or the adults dealing with it consider it racist or not.

The official definition of a racist incident is this: 'Any incident which is perceived to be racist by the victim or any other person.' The term 'racism' refers to conduct or words or practices that disadvantage or advantage people because of their colour, culture or ethnic origin. A useful working definition in schools is 'behaviour or language that makes a pupil feel unwelcome or marginalised because of their colour, ethnicity, culture, religion or national origin' (Stephen Lawrence Inquiry, Chapter 47, Recommendation 12).

A racist insult may refer to issues of culture or religion as well as to colour and appearance. Records should be kept of incidents in school and on journeys to and from school and reported to the local authority on their standard form. This racist incident log will also be looked at by school inspectors.

Some of your pupils from ethnic minorities will have English as an additional language. Some of them may be on the first level (of three) of language acquisition. These are the ones who are readily identified and provision is made for. With scarce resources, what is your school doing to make sure that the higher level EAL pupils are making as much progress as they should? Although pupils pick up conversational English quickly, researchers say that it takes between five and seven years to have an equal grasp of academic written English. Tenses may be confused, subtleties in meaning overlooked or sentence construction might be unorthodox. How is the English department addressing this? Is an extra class necessary? What support does your local authority give?

As I said earlier, ethos is about the underlying sentiments that guide beliefs, customs and practices. You can establish these by carefully selecting staff, modelling, training and putting inclusive routines and systems into practice. Ensure that different groups of pupils are all given responsibilities and opportunities to take part in activities. Assemblies are a good opportunity to reinforce your ideals, and there are lots of good ideas at www.globalgateway.co.uk. What will you celebrate in your school? High results? Achievement? Participation? Attendance? Personal development? Why not all of them? Don't forget to do it in front of parents, governors and the outside world as often as possible. They are your public relations.

Good schools are where:

- Pupils are involved in mediating in disputes, and in making clear that racist remarks and behaviour are unacceptable. Pupils support each other in being assertive, as distinct from aggressive or submissive, when incidents occur.
- All staff are vigilant with regard to behaviour among pupils, and have some understanding of pupils' experiences of bullying and racist incidents.
- Pupils have opportunities to report racist incidents anonymously.
- There are periodic surveys of pupils' experiences and perceptions of racism, using questionnaires and discussion groups, and involving people from outside the school if appropriate.
- Staff accept that they have a responsibility to ensure that play and leisure areas encourage and promote positive and co-operative behaviour among pupils.
- The general ethos of the school (displays, assemblies, the examples chosen across the curriculum) reflects and affirms diversity of language, culture, religion and appearance. See the Qualification and Curriculum Authority's 'Respect for All' website for examples across the curriculum at www.qca.org.uk/qca_6753.aspx. It includes an audit tool for your school.
- The school is involved from time to time in national projects such as Kick Racism Out of Football, One World Week, Black History Month, Islamic Awareness Week and Refugee Week.
- PSHE/Citizenship includes coverage of the different ways racism can sometimes subtly show itself, besides racist name-calling and bullying, and links are made to wider issues.

Chapter 4

Organisation
Budgets and staffing

Where does your budget come from?

Funding arrangements for schools changed in 2008. Budgets are now allocated to schools to cover three years, which allows a certain amount of stability. The current round is April 2008–11. Match your financial planning for inclusion to that.

How does the money filter down? The government decides how much the Dedicated Schools Grant should be for each local authority. They use a formula to determine how much additional money should go to areas of deprivation.

Local authorities

Local authorities decide how much of their resources to spend on education and, within that, how much to spend on pupil provision in the Schools Budget. The local authority consults with the local Schools Forum about how much of the Schools Budget to pass to individual schools according to their level of deprivation (there are government guidelines), government priorities, and how much to keep back centrally. Central budgets vary among local authorities but can cover elements of special educational needs such as support teams. Some money – for example, the Ethnic Minority Achievement Grant (EMAG) – is ring-fenced, meaning it can only be used for that purpose.

From time to time there is extra money for government initiatives. For example, the Standards Fund 2006–8 was targeted at schools facing challenges and wanting to develop personalised learning. There were no specific conditions attached to this money, although the DfES suggested projects it might fund, such as:

* transitions;
* small group teaching, or 1:1;
* gifted and talented;
* assessment for learning;
* making smaller sets and teaching groups;
* study support;
* interventions for potential underperformers such as certain ethnic minorities, white British boys, SEN and looked-after children;
* information on progress to parents;
* training.

Your local authority receives a block of money from the Children's Fund. Local authorities are expected to use this money strategically to support the Every Child Matters agenda, not just to support particularly vulnerable children. What is your local authority providing? Details of funding going to schools from central government can be found at www.teachernet.gov.uk/management/schoolfunding/schoolfunding2008to11. The money is given in three-year blocks to allow better strategic planning. If you go to the website http://ygt.dcsf.gov.uk – the Young, Gifted and Talented site – there you'll find a friendlier explanation of available grants, including those aimed at vulnerable children not exclusively gifted and talented. Search the catalogue on the site for Useful Links, Funding, then click on Standards Fund grants 2008–11.

About half of English schools are 'extended schools' in one way or another, providing personalised learning with study support, referral to support services and activities to motivate pupils and raise achievement. Some do it in partnership with their local authority, local schools, or the private or voluntary sector. Getting involved with extended services may sound like working an 18-hour day for the same salary, but the idea is to minimise burdens on headteachers and staff by sharing the workload. Many schools have used the funding to set up breakfast or homework clubs and catch-up classes.

Guidance on becoming and running an extended school is at www.teachernet.gov.uk/wholeschool/extendedschools/practicalknowhow/. Talk to parents and get them involved from the beginning.

Learning and Skills Council

The Learning and Skills Council (LSC) is responsible for funding and planning education and training for over-16-year-olds in England. You will find more information on the LSC at www.lsc.gov.uk.

The role of school governors

The governing body is responsible for deciding how to spend the individual school's budget to ensure that resources are allocated in line with agreed priorities and will deliver value for money. To demonstrate value for money for SEN, the Audit Commission website at http://sen-aen.audit-commission.gov.uk may be helpful.

The governors also review progress to make sure that spending is delivering the right results and keeps within budget limits. Under the new funding arrangements from 2008, the local authority can claw back 'excessive' revenue balances and redistribute these to other schools. 'Excessive' means a carryover of more than 5 per cent in secondary schools or 8 per cent in primary.

Day-to-day financial decisions are generally delegated to the headteacher. Schools are not obliged to publish accounts. However, they must produce a financial statement as part of the governors' report at their Annual General Meeting. In the past, it was notoriously difficult to find out about what money came into your school for inclusion, and hence what might be available for any initiatives you had in mind. Some of the money is earmarked. For example, there is a specific formula grant to pay for the introduction of diplomas at Key Stage 4. The governors and headteacher can use their discretion for most of the funding. The SEN Code of Practice says the cost of the Special

Educational Needs Co-ordinator should come from the school's basic budget and not out of money allocated for SEN/LDD.

Other sources of income

The website www.teachernet.gov.uk/management/atoz/search/index.cfm may point you in the direction of funding sources you didn't know about. Money should be used to further the school development plan. You have to bid for some resources so it should be for those that have priority in your SDP or inclusion plan. You might also find the following potential sources of funding useful:

- Heritage Lottery Fund
- the Comenius and Leonardo da Vinci programmes of the European Union
- the Single Regeneration budget
- New Deal for Communities
- sponsorship.

Your School Improvement Partner may also point you in the direction of other sources. Many of these will be time-limited, so it is important to plan ahead to make sure you can sustain what you start. Schools are expected to charge for all childcare and study support, but also to ensure there is free access to study support for pupils who have fallen behind. Many schools operate a separate tariff for identified groups.

Until the end of the 2007/8 academic year, there was money available under the Schools Access Initiative for physical adaptations to schools: £20m for voluntary aided schools and £80m for mainstream. Schools applied via their local authority, who also have some funding for this. More details are at www.teachernet.gov.uk/management/resourcesfinanceandbuilding/FSP/sai.

Funding for statemented pupils

Your local authority (or adjoining authorities who send pupils to your school) will delegate money for each child with a statement of special educational need and those at School Action Plus. This will probably be linked to a 'matrix of need' for each pupil so that schools are treated equally. The local authority should also clarify which elements should be met from maintained schools' budgets and which ones should come from the central local authority budget. The more severe the disability, the higher the funding. Funding follows the pupil so that pupils transferring from a special school will bring in extra income. Your headteacher, bursar and local-authority SEN officer will know how much this is, because it varies quite dramatically between local authorities.

Local authorities should monitor casual admissions with respect to pupils' SEN and try to ensure that schools that take on pupils mid-year are given the necessary financial resources or specialist support.

Provision mapping

This is a useful tool for planning provision and should be at least an annual exercise. A provision map identifies additional or different provision and its cost. If you are new to the job or the local authority, you will need to find out what services are available and which ones are funded centrally. Some local authorities have a handbook, or you may prefer to link with another school to find this out. You can employ people outside the usual 'education' network, such as a psychotherapist. One example of unorthodox provision is where local football teams run literacy classes alongside sporting opportunities. By putting all the provision on paper (or a spreadsheet), you will be able to spot any gaps in what you offer.

A provision map links provision to individuals so that you can see what an individual pupil has had over time. It will help you identify repetitive or ineffective use of resources.

Table 4.1 Provision mapping

Year group 7	Provision	Group/Individual	Cost in time and staff per week
A. Einstein W. Churchill S. Redgrave T. Cruise W. Disney	Phonics group spelling in registration	Group of 5 × 2	2 × 15 mins TA
	Paired reading with 6th form	15 pairs in 3 groups	2 × 20mins SENCO 2 × 20 mins TA
	Speech and language therapy	Group (4) Individual (2)	1 × 20 mins SALT 2 × 15 mins SALT 1 × 30 mins TA

You could include on the record individual pupils' targets and outcomes so that you can use it as a tool in reviews. By having this information in one central source, you can more easily report to governors on the success of the SEN policy, see patterns and plan developments. By adding costings to the provision, you are not only demonstrating accountability but it also makes you aware of what provision is value for money. By stepping back like this from individual provision to a systematic look, it helps focus attention on whole-school issues of teaching and learning rather than individual timetables.

There is no definitive layout for a provision map. Maps can be done by key stage or year group, by 'wave' of support or by type of provision, such as Cognition and Learning. Beware of the last type since many pupils are difficult to pigeonhole. That way of drawing the provision map works well if you simply want to show the range of provision. Essentially, the format is down to whatever works for your school. It is easier to leave the cost in terms of time and staffing than to work out in money terms as salaries change.

This can help you budget but also work out what is 'best value'. For example, if you were considering continuing literacy withdrawal lessons for small groups in Year 8 with a teaching assistant, you might look at last term's provision map then consider the 'four C's':

• *Challenge*: Do you really need this provision? What are pupils gaining from these sessions? What effect is it having on the subjects they are withdrawn from?

- *Consult*: What do the pupils think about it? What do their subject teachers and parents think?
- *Compare*: How does pupils' progress compare with national figures? How does it compare with pupils who have not had this provision?
- *Compete*: Is it cost-effective? Can you get better results in a shorter time with bought-in specialist teaching or by employing extra staff to provide smaller sets in English?

Provision mapping can provide uncomfortable data because it is often the first time the costings have been worked out. This can be a threat to centrally funded teams who are bought in, who appear to be expensive but are bringing considerable expertise to a school population, whose needs may be different next term.

Remember that you identify need first and match provision to it. You are not looking at provision and finding pupils to fill it. The main question you should be asking is 'Does additional support lead to sustained improvement for pupils?' If it doesn't, why are you continuing with it? There has been research on what literacy interventions work best in primary schools. This very useful report, published in 2007, is at www.standards. dcsf/gov.uk/primary/publications/literacy.

Look for alternatives.

Staffing

This is where more than 80 per cent of the school's budget goes. Together with the quality of leadership and management, the quality of teaching will determine, more than any other factor, how well your pupils achieve. Your school's checks on employment will show what teaching qualifications your staff have. Do you know what else they can do? Have they got another language or a specialist qualification? Are they interested in developing a specialism? As long as they are good quality, a stable staff means that you can have continuity in planning and you have time to develop their strengths.

Start at the basics.

Making the most of your team's talents

Do staff have access to:

- food, water and a break during the day? (We tend to forget these.)
- bookable pleasant rooms where they can talk in confidence to parents, pupils and other professionals?
- enough telephones? Can outside calls get through easily, or do office staff pass on accurate messages promptly?
- computers and central records of pupils?
- annual child-protection training?

Do staff have:

- an up-to-date job description?
- clear line management, supervision and regular reviews of their performance linked to continuing professional development?

- pay when they go on training courses?
- a period of induction and a mentor?
- the chance to discuss case studies and swap expertise in a structured way?
- opportunities to talk about lesson plans and evaluate them?
- a fair salary structure?

Do all of these apply to you?

In the case of the Inclusion Manager, there are no rules on funding, but it is salutary to check what your role has been over the term and highlight any tasks that could have been delegated to named others. Work out what proportion of your time has been spent on:

- administration
- coaching, mentoring and advising staff
- whole-school/departmental training
- in-school meetings
- meeting and talking with parents
- meeting outside professionals
- tracking progress
- quality assurance
- planning
- other.

Do all of these need your high-level strategic input or can you safely delegate?

Staff deployment is aimed at increasing the inclusion of particular pupils or groups and raising their achievement to the level of their peers. Your school may employ a SENCO, specialist teachers, therapists, learning mentors, or teaching assistants. Your office staff and lunchtime supervisors will also have a role in ensuring inclusion. It is important that these roles are well defined and that they do not overlap. Their job descriptions should include having a part to play in policy development.

What to look for in a SENCO

Under proposals announced in October 2006, all Special Educational Needs Co-ordinators have to be qualified teachers, and from 2009, will have to complete a nationally accredited qualification that will cover the most common problems and contact details for expert organisations. The chart below is based on the Training and Development Agency for Schools list of attributes, skills and knowledge that they expect to be the minimum requirements for a SENCO. More details of the requirements are at www.tda.gov.uk/upload/resources/pdf/s/senco_spec.

The chart can be used for SENCOs to self-audit, to help prepare questions for interview and selection, and can be used in performance review. In recent years, there was a drift towards appointing teaching assistants as SENCOs, but although there are administrative routines that can be carried out by them, they were not likely to have the qualities, knowledge and ability to influence and manage staff across the school. When the SEN Code of Practice was published in 2001, it assumed the SENCO would be a teacher.

The following aspects of special needs work that can be effectively done by support staff. How far you extend these responsibilities depends obviously on the quality of your staff.

- Linking with staff, other agencies and parents.
- Running clubs.
- Organising and using assistive technology.
- Working with departments to adapt materials with direction from a teacher.
- Producing and disseminating paperwork and emails.
- Keeping track of resources.
- Working with individuals and small groups on ready-made specific interventions, such as booster sessions or speech and language programmes after training by a therapist.

The day-to-day direction of staff and resources, identification of pupils with special educational needs and meeting the needs of those pupils are the responsibilities of the SENCO. Here is a suggested tick list for the SENCO to complete (Table 4.2). This could be used for reflecting on practice by the SENCO, or as a basis for a performance-management conversation, to identify training needs.

Table 4.2 SENCO competency checklist

SENCO competency	Good at this	Need to develop
Know the characteristics of effective teaching		
Use ICT effectively		
Keep up to date with inclusion and SEN issues and interventions		
Effective communication		
Co-ordinate and provide staff training		
Manage Individual Education Plans		
Collect, analyse and interpret assessment data		
Assist staff to set realistic expectations		
Disseminate good practice		
Monitor and evaluate the provision for pupils with SEN, including the effectiveness of teaching and learning		
Support literacy, numeracy, ICT and other developments		
Support pupils to become independent learners		
Manage transitions effectively		
Devise, implement and evaluate SEN systems		
Provide regular information for senior leadership and governing body on the effectiveness of SEN provision		
Help staff understand the needs of pupils with SEN and provide training		
Promote and achieve positive staff/pupil relationships		
Monitor pupil progress		
Co-ordinate reviews		
Develop positive partnerships with parents		
Develop effectives liaison with other agencies		
Chair meetings effectively		
Manage time effectively		
Take responsibility for own professional development		

From Ann Sydney (2010) *A Handbook for Inclusion Managers*, London: Routledge. © 2010 Ann Sydney

Some forward-thinking schools have appointed Curriculum Support Teachers in each key stage. They are experienced in teaching pupils with a range of severe disabilities. Reporting to the SENCO or Inclusion Manager, their job is to ensure that the curriculum is differentiated for pupils with severe disabilities by looking at teachers' planning and making suggestions and modifications for pupils with particular needs. This gives teachers confidence and support. Sometimes they observe lessons or train teaching assistants. They look at notes from teaching assistants and meet teachers regularly to assess how successful the modifications have been. This works well in primary schools where a pupil with additional needs has only one or two teachers, but it could also be adapted in secondary by having link teachers in some departments.

What to look for in a teaching assistant

The following are important skills and characteristics to look for in a teaching assistant:

- good basic skills in literacy, numeracy and ICT;
- a commitment to inclusion;
- discretion, an understanding of confidentiality;
- an interest in further training;
- good non-confrontational communication skills;
- flexibility, willingness to support the whole range of pupils;
- willingness to take responsibility, such as for working with small groups in the classroom.

With new teaching assistants, it is helpful to give them induction that involves training, followed by experience supporting a high-quality TA, then the responsibility of working alone with the chance to ask for advice. They need time to read and prepare before they take on a full-time role. They should have copies of the schemes of work, pupils' targets and any modified materials. They can be attached to:

- pupils or tutor groups
- subject areas
- key stages.

Most statements will say how much teaching assistant time is to be allocated to the pupil. This must be complied with first before you do any other deployment. Ensure that trained and experienced support staff are working with the most complex pupils. If you have two statemented pupils in one class, you do not necessarily need to have two TAs supporting. Even with a TA 'attached' to a pupil, this does not mean that they should be sitting with them all the time, taking notes for them or doing the work. This is unrewarding for the TA, isolating for the pupil, and there are other ways of recording information. Rather than working 1:1 in class with a pupil, where the pupil necessarily becomes more isolated from the rest of the class, the TA could work with a small group including the targeted pupil. Pupils on the autistic spectrum or those with specific medical needs may need to have more stable allocation of staff, but it need not necessarily be just one person. Teaching assistants should keep records of pupils' response to the work so that it can be better matched another time. At those times when the class teacher is teaching from the front of the class, the teaching assistant could be recording how often pupils with additional needs are involved in the lesson. Records could be written discreetly in a notebook to supplement verbal feedback to the class teacher at the end of the lesson, if there is time.

Many schools find there is an advantage in attaching some teaching assistants to departments. This way they can be involved in curricular information, planning materials and lessons. One benefit of such an arrangement is that pupils do not become reliant, even dependent, on a particular teaching assistant. Whichever method or mix you choose, it is important that the class teacher briefs any additional adults in class about their role, lesson objectives, and how they can best support which pupils. They can have a variety of roles, including modelling, signing, scribing, or observing; what they are not is another member of the class listening to the lesson. They can be very useful in carrying out behaviour programmes. As part of this, they could be systematically observing behaviour on different occasions and feeding this back to the pupil and teacher.

An example of this is below in Table 4.3. Each box is an interval of ten seconds. Scan the room so that it is not clear who you are watching, then mark the box each time. Do it for about ten minutes. Make a note of the circumstances – lesson, seating, time of day. You could track two very different pupils in different colours on the same chart. This is just an example and would be part of a wider behaviour programme where the SENCO might identify the pupil's good points and problems, prioritise one problem, describe what the pupils should be doing instead, plan steps to achieve a SMART (specific, measurable, achievable, reasonable, time-limited) target, and decide on changes to the antecedents and consequences of the behaviour. Changes might involve parents, teachers and other pupils. This chart would be useful in identifying what triggers and follows particular behaviour. Feeding the evidence back dispassionately to the pupil can be a revelation to them. If you have a Behaviour Support Team or adviser, they can suggest ways to develop this.

Where specialist teachers, learning mentors and teaching assistants are withdrawing pupils from lessons, this should be part of a time-limited intervention that does not take them out of the same lesson each week. Eight weeks of an intervention should be enough time to see if it is working and worth continuing, working well enough to return pupils to class, or not working and something else needs to be tried.

It is important that teaching assistants are involved in performance management and in the lesson-monitoring cycle. While you will get some useful information from class teachers about the effectiveness of support in class, some focussed lesson observations

Table 4.3 Behaviour checklist for teaching assistants

	10	20	30	40	50	00	10	20	30	40	50	00	10	20	30	40	50
On task	/	/	/		/		/										
Talking				/		/											
Looking																	
Movement																	
Fidgeting																	
Making noise												/					
Teacher interaction						/			/		/			/	/		
Other							/			/						/	/

(they only need to be half an hour) will give you information you can feed back to the TA and feed in to the training cycle.

Higher Level Teaching Assistants

Higher Level Teaching Assistants (HLTAs) are only found in England. The headteacher and line manager (probably you) have to give support to anyone wishing to train and be assessed as an HLTA. There are literacy and numeracy requirements for the course. Applications are made via the local authority, who use funding from the Teacher Development Agency. If you work in a non-maintained school, you need to apply to a Regional Provider of Assessment. RPA contact lists are on the HLTA part of the Training and Development Agency website at www.tda.gov.uk/support/hlta/becomingahlta/funding.aspx.

What to look for in staff linking with special schools

Generally it is staff from special schools who are bringing in their specialist knowledge and support rather than mainstream staff linking with special schools. The South West Regional Partnership handbook at www.sw-special.co.uk has very useful information on co-working. When pupils are transferring from special school to mainstream, perhaps with needs you have not met before, you need to identify some mainstream staff who will lead the way. They should be:

* positive and enthusiastic about inclusion;
* a problem-solver;
* someone with influence in the mainstream school, and who has the ear of the leadership team;
* a good practitioner, able to adapt lessons creatively;
* a good communicator, who can spread a positive message among your staff;
* someone who is willing to visit the link special school and take advice from staff at all levels;
* someone with high expectations of all pupils;
* skilled in behaviour management.

What to look for in a learning mentor

A learning mentor is not a teacher but acts as a role model, listener and guide for pupils. Learning mentors help plan support and negotiate targets for pupils. Learning mentors forge links with parents and outside agencies. They are not expected to keep discipline in class, nor are they trained counsellors, although some do choose to train. Learning mentors have proved successful in motivating pupils, improving attendance and reducing exclusion. There are excellent guidelines for learning mentors at www.standards.dfes.gov.uk/sie/documents/LMGoodPractGuide.pdf and at www.standards.dfes.gov.uk/learningmentors.
    Learning mentors need to:

* be good listeners;
* respect confidentiality inside and outside school, and be trained in child protection;

- be prepared to make warm non-confrontational relationships with difficult pupils;
- be emotionally resilient;
- be proactive;
- be prepared to learn new skills.

It also helps if they are from a similar background to the pupils they are supporting.

As the Inclusion Manager, your job will be to ensure that learning mentors have a distinct role in the pastoral system, and that all staff are aware of it. You should identify any groups that you expect learning mentors to be supporting. Referral and, equally importantly, exit criteria need to be established and known. In some schools, learning mentors' line management is as unclear to them as it is to the rest of the staff. Line management needs to be clear-cut, and there needs to be frequent access to managers. Learning mentors have a valuable role in any reviews and multi-agency meetings, and for this reason, they will need to keep clear, discreet records. Schools use learning mentors in a variety of ways: for group work in social skills or anger management, circle time, running clubs or working in the Learning Support Centre. Most of their work will be 1:1, providing an ear for troubled and troubling pupils and helping with target-setting. They can be extremely useful at times of choice and transition, including for mid-phase entrants, refugees and asylum seekers.

What to look for in the mirror

Inclusion Managers need:

- to keep abreast of what is available;
- a strategic view of what is needed to raise achievement of all groups;
- good networks beyond school;
- the ability to identify new opportunities even if they are not innovators themselves;
- determination to continually raise the quality of provision;
- leadership qualities to take staff, parents and other professionals along with them;
- clear written and verbal communication;
- expectation of different types of achievement: a balance of academic, vocational and personal and social;
- a life beyond school;
- resilience and optimism to deal with the workload.

And they should not give off even the faintest whiff of burning martyr . . .

Training links

What opportunities are there for you to train staff? The school's professional development cycle should include inclusion training for the head and leadership team, middle managers, class teachers, teaching assistants and other adults working in the school. In a secondary school, you may also have an Inclusion Committee with a member drawn from each faculty, which can revise policies as well as being a conduit for information and training.

Communicating

It is no good having a wealth of data and information to identify and assess pupils if it stays in your filing cabinet. Most schools have an intranet where all this can be shared. Make sure your network manager uploads it as 'read only' so that it cannot be changed. You might limit access to some information. Consider putting student profiles on the system: a description of pupils' strengths and weaknesses, needs, provision, preferred learning style, and tips for behaviour management. Highlight those pupils on the SEN register. These could be added to the standard whole-school data of Cognitive Assessment Tests and Standard Assessment Test scores, any individual test scores for reading, spelling and maths, subject levels, Fischer Family Trust predictions and a colour-coded alert system for when pupils are not achieving these. Having an easy way of communicating on the intranet will help when you need to gather information before reviews or to see patterns in pupil achievement. Be aware of the Data Protection Act and confidentiality. There is a readable summary for schools on the Becta website at http://schools.becta. org.uk in the Leadership and Management section, and Becta produce a useful document, 'Data Protection and Security: A summary for schools'. Reduce bureaucracy by having pre-populated forms and by cutting out any duplication; for example, have a single plan for each child on the SEN register, and fit the SEN targets into the same system as other pupils have for their academic targets.

You do not need to have a hand in every aspect of inclusion. Build a team around you comprising staff from a cross-section of the school and different levels of seniority so each can feed back to their own team/faculty. This way, responsibility is shared and people are accountable. You will also get information from a number of points of view. Set up regular meetings so that everyone is informed, but keep meetings to strict time limits.

Celebrate the good news in your school. You will soon lose support in the staffroom if staff see you as always demanding and being critical. Make sure you sell your role as one that benefits staff as well as pupils. Involve staff in determining:

- what information helps teachers to track progress;
- how it is best collected, shared and analysed;
- how this can lead on to a better match between lesson plans and pupils' needs.

Chapter 5

Curriculum

From September 2002, the Disability Discrimination Act 1995 was extended to cover education, obliging schools to take reasonable steps to ensure that disabled pupils are not disadvantaged in any area of school life. Access to the full and extended curriculum is governed by this amendment. The National Curriculum has an inclusion statement at the front of each subject booklet. There has recently been a move towards personalisation of the curriculum for all pupils, and a greater degree of flexibility at all key stages, leading to some schools covering Key Stage 3 in two years, with early entry to GCSE, or vocational courses in school and off-site. Some schools have responded to this flexibility by looking at their own particular needs, whether this is teaching Bengali, Mandarin or British Sign Language instead of a modern foreign language; teaching philosophy as a way of improving thinking skills (see, for example, www.sapere.net); having an extension of the primary curriculum in Year 7, such as the Royal Society of Arts 'Opening Minds' life skills curriculum for all Year 7 pupils; or providing catch-up classes for absentees. Some networks of schools join together to provide vocational courses or swap specialist teachers and resources for part of the week. Think creatively.

For pupils who are struggling academically, there is a whole range of ways a school can intervene. Here is a selection of ideas, many of them from the National Strategy:

- summer schools;
- improving curriculum continuity between key stages;
- literacy progress units;
- springboard maths;
- critical teaching units in English and maths (for example, to lift Year 7 pupils from Level 3 to Level 4);
- the Learning Challenge (KS3 & 4) catch-up and study skills in reading, writing and maths;
- science intervention for pupils struggling to move from Level 4 to Level 5;
- Year 9 booster lessons;
- academic or learning mentors;
- Access & Engagement in science/English/maths for English-as-an-additional-language learners. These are part of the KS3 Strategy and suggest teaching strategies for pupils at different stages of EAL.

Gifted and talented pupils

The usual definition of gifted is 'academically very able', and talented means 'advanced in one or more artistic or sporting areas'. The government expect there to be 5 to 10 per cent of pupils in each school who are achieving, or have the potential to achieve, significantly in advance of their year group. The Young Gifted and Talented (YG&T) programme started a new phase in September 2007. Each maintained school and college has a nominated lead teacher for gifted and talented. A new Learner Academy has been set up nationally, aimed at the top 10 per cent of pupils, not just in traditional school subjects but also in vocational, leadership, entrepreneurial and cross-curricular skills. The contracted company is linking with universities and other providers nationally to provide resources and enrichment activities. Online resources are aimed at improving practice in the classroom so that all learners, not just the most able, can benefit. The best introduction is the portal at www.ygt.dcsf.gov.uk, which provides lots of links. Probably the first place to look if you have overall responsibility is the Quality Standards part of the site. This is a range of self-evaluation tools that look at whole-school provision as well as planning at the classroom level. In a pilot project in 2006/7, schools found the tools very valuable: they fed into their school self-evaluation (and Self-Evaluation Form) and strategic planning. They were a vehicle for bringing staff together to discuss current and future provision and to develop a policy. Schools reported an impact on attainment, attendance and school ethos. The website also has resources, case studies and schemes of work as well as a source of funding via the Sutton Trust link.

The education of the most able pupils has gone through several models. The idea of picking out one in five or ten in every school and offering special classes has its weaknesses, particularly in a selective school system. The Eppi Centre report 2008 (http://eppi.ioe.ac.uk/cms/Default.aspx?tabid=2402) says that able children thrive when they manage their own learning. Rather than offer a separate provision to an elite few, they suggest that thinking skills, an enriched curriculum and personalised provision are more effective. Schools have found that focusing on personalised learning, having good assessment procedures, using tracking to identify talent and ability, providing enrichment activities and matching the curriculum to pupils' interests raise the achievement of all pupils. Some schools enter pupils for exams by ability rather than age. Extension activities which are demanding puzzles, open-ended tasks, and problem-solving exercises motivate able pupils, rather than more of the same work. Enrichment activities can come from the talents of staff in the school, parents or outside agencies. A good example is the National Space Centre in Leicester, which, like many museums, runs not only workshops but also outreach and videoconferencing with schools across the country.

You may have a Gifted and Talented Co-ordinator who takes on this oversight. Without one, and as a member of the senior management team, you need to check that the curriculum and timetable are flexible and creative. Communicate with pupils to find what they want and, later, what works, and communicate this to staff.

Naturally, the impact of anything you introduce to school has to be evaluated – through lesson observation, by talking to pupils to gauge their motivation and achievement, through getting feedback from parents and staff and, importantly, by tracking achievement and attendance.

Distance learning

You may need to consider distance learning for pupils with poor attendance, including some Gypsy, Roma and traveller pupils and those with medical needs. How do you support children when they are not in school? You may have catch-up classes after school when they do attend, but how do you keep pupils motivated and achieving if they have intermittent attendance? In 2007, about 200 pupils in England were using laptops and data cards linked to a mobile phone network. Most of these were primary pupils linking to one teacher in school. In secondary schools, this way of working will involve several specialist staff working with each pupil. This needs to be organised systematically rather than relying on the commitment of particular teachers. The introduction of virtual learning platforms should go some way toward solving the problem of intermittent attenders, allowing pupils and their parents access to the school network from home. There are also commercial packages such as www.inonit.lgfl.net, covering Foundation Stage to Key Stage 4 in all subjects apart from PE, and www.notschool.net for Key Stage 4 pupils.

In the case of Gypsy, Roma and traveller pupils, the big question is not just 'How do you provide a worthwhile education for pupils with poor/irregular/seasonal attendance?' but 'How do you provide a curriculum that acknowledges and reflects the needs of their culture?' There are several references in the further reading section at the back of this book that may help.

Do you already identify gaps in pupils' education? Can your curriculum be flexible enough to fill in these gaps? At secondary level, are there courses that it is possible to dip in and out of, or are they all progressive? Traditionally the travelling community have valued working at an early age. In 2007, the West Midlands Consortium for the Education of Traveller Children piloted a new approach at Key Stage 4, using an informal apprenticeship model for vocational education. It focuses on challenges that are relevant and capture the interest of young travellers and build up their skills in working together and problem-solving. Accreditation could be through Award Scheme Development and Accreditation Network (ASDAN)/Certificate of Personal Effectiveness (COPE). Remember this is one option; individual pupils may have their sights set differently.

Funding went from the government to local authorities in 2006–8 for Computers for Pupils to ensure that poorer pupils have computers at home that the whole family can benefit from. The money went to the 20 per cent most deprived local authorities according to a formula, and they agree with their schools how it should be allocated. Schools need to have 30 or more pupils in Key Stages 3 and 4 eligible for free school meals (FSM). No bidding is required. Some funding for connectivity is included for the first year. 'When deciding on the priorities and final allocation of the Computers for Pupils funding, schools and local authorities should take into account their duty to promote equality and also ensure they do not, either deliberately or unwittingly, discriminate against any particular group on the grounds of race, gender or disability' (Becta, 'Computers for Pupils and Access to Technology at Home', chapter 3.11). There are, of course, some things to consider if you are in the lucky situation of having funding in your school; the equipment, including any assistive technology, belongs to the school, so you need a home-school agreement setting out responsibilities, purpose of the long-term loan, virus protection, maintenance and return of the equipment. Some hurdles might be insurance, where the neediest families are unable to afford or get coverage, paying for connectivity after the first year, and keeping contact with travelling families.

The Teachernet website has updates on the scheme, and a report on a promising pilot is at www.schmoller.net/documents/elamps-1.doc.

Self-evaluation criteria for the curriculum

'Special Educational Needs and Disability: Towards inclusive schools' DfES 2004 suggests the following:

- There is sensitive allocation to teaching groups and careful modification of the curriculum, timetables and social arrangements. Spread your needy pupils among classes, though having two supported pupils with similar needs in one class can lead to more efficient deployment of teaching assistants.
- The pupils whose reading ages fall below their peers have access to special help. This doesn't have to mean withdrawal classes during lesson time.
- The curriculum is reviewed annually in the light of a regular audit of pupils' needs, and the school responds to the outcomes of the review by establishing additional and/or different programmes of study to meet their needs
- Plans to innovate the curriculum to give greater access are included in the school disability access plan. (This plan refers to curriculum access as much as to ramps and rails.)
- The school monitors option choices, work experience, vocational choices and the provision of appropriate pathways and accreditation.

There is a great deal of flexibility in the school curriculum at Key Stage 4, so that college links and work placements can be established to provide a more personalised curriculum. The idea of 'studio schools' for small groups of pupils attached to businesses and vocational workshops is being discussed at the time of writing (2008).

Careers and vocational guidance should be available to all pupils in secondary school in Year 7, so that by KS4, pupils have a high but realistic view of what they can aim for based on thorough information. All pupils should be involved in worthwhile work experience. The easy option with some pupils with disabilities is to let them do work experience in the school office or nursery, but they need the opportunity to experience a completely different setting and people – just like everybody else, but possibly with more support.

Do pupils from minority ethnic groups, pupils in care, gifted and talented, young carers or those with special educational needs attend clubs, including homework and revision clubs? If they are under-represented, what is preventing them? It might have something to do with travel arrangements that can be changed, or the timing and range of clubs being too narrow. Similarly, are all groups represented on outings, including residential trips? If not, why?

Language across the curriculum

Does your school have a policy on language development? This is important not just for pupils for whom English is an additional language, but for those pupils with inadequate language skills who may react instead with poor behaviour, and for those with speech and communication difficulties. Language is fundamental to a sense of self and belonging as well as to achievement. Many schools with pupils underachieving in writing or with poor behaviour go one step back in the development process and look at speaking and listening as the key to improvement. Where you have pupils with significant learning difficulties, you may consider introducing symbols or objects of reference. Special school staff will be able to advise on how to go about this. Software such as Writing with Symbols (commonly referred to as Widgit) is available from www.widgit.com. This will enable you to produce teaching materials and visual timetables. It might also support pupils with English as an additional language. It is possible to make dual-language talking books with software called Clicker, available from www.cricksoft.com, and the help of a home-language speaker.

Your language policy should state:

* that you value languages equally and how you demonstrate this;
* what support you give;
* that all staff have responsibility for developing pupils' skills in written as well as spoken English;
* that there is an acknowledgement that academic written English takes a long time to acquire and is a long-term commitment;
* that teachers have had training in developing language in the classroom;
* that pupils learn about different types of writing for different purposes and become familiar with nuances in spoken and written English throughout school.

The role of the Learning Support Unit

The 'Excellence in Cities' programme from the late 1990s included funding for setting up Learning Support Units, though many schools had similar provision long before this called by another name. In my son's secondary school, it was known as 'Room 101'. The school has moved on a long way from there. The government provided 'Good Practice Guidelines for Learning Support Units' (DfES 2002) based on research in LSUs. It found they had the following impact:

* Attendance improved.
* Truancy decreased.
* Exclusions decreased.
* Staying-on rates in secondary improved.
* Pupils gained more qualifications and basic skills improved.
* Behaviour around the school improved.
* Pupils had higher confidence and self-esteem.
* Transitions went more smoothly.
* There were better relationships and more contact with parents.

So what are the features of good Learning Support Units that produce these minor miracles?

* They have small classes, often with a degree of 1:1 teaching.
* Staff have more detailed information about the pupils' progress and academic and behavioural difficulties.

- Staff have more confidence in dealing with difficult behaviour as a result of training.
- Outside agencies are targeted more effectively.
- There is more use of flexible curriculum packages.

All of these factors might be replicated on a whole-school scale.

There are very effective Learning Support Units in both primary and secondary schools where the intervention is short term and there are clear entry and exit strategies and criteria. They focus on teaching and reinforcing skills required for pupils to participate more effectively within lessons. The aim is always to reintegrate the pupil into mainstream class. What the effective ones also have in common is trained staff who link well with mainstream teachers, and premises that are attractive, well resourced and are an integral part of the school. Staff provide behaviour and curriculum packages that are tailored to individual pupils. For example, in a primary unit, pupils play with sand, water and miniature worlds, initially with an adult who stimulates their language skills, then gradually spending time in parallel play before moving on to co-operative play. There is a mix of teacher-directed and pupil-initiated work, reminiscent of what you would see in Early Years. Essentially, the LSU is filling in the gaps in pupils' development so that they can benefit from mainstream primary, where they gradually spend more time. A fundamental feature is clear and detailed record keeping, not just of pupils' achievements and academic difficulties, but also the behaviour triggers and responses. Pupils who have been reintegrated still come back to show 'good work' and are able to have drop-in counseling. Parents drop by at the start and end of the day, and there are home-school books that keep everyone informed. Some pupils will be working in the LSU while they are being formally assessed for a statement of special educational need, and the detailed record keeping will feed into this process.

The worst case scenario for a Learning Support Unit might be that it is in a building isolated from the rest of the school, with shabby accommodation, where none of the pupils join the rest of the school even at break times. It is run by untrained learning support assistants (LSAs) who are kind and hardworking but are learning on the job without the support of any specialist teachers. Pupils are referred there for a wide variety of reasons and do not know how long they will be there, or what needs to happen for them to return to class. Some are the victims of bullying that has not been effectively addressed, hence the separate playtimes. Some pupils may have dyslexia or dyspraxia, and their specialist needs are not met. Resources are old-fashioned and sparse. Some school staff send work, which is invariably note taking and worksheets, so pupils are essentially being deprived of teaching. No proper data is kept on the progress of pupils who are there or have been there. Older pupils miss so much of the mainstream curriculum that they are seriously disadvantaged when/if they take examinations.

Learning Support Units are not a long-term replacement for pupils who need a more specialist setting, nor are they where to send challenging pupils just before they are excluded. They should be provided at one stage of a behaviour policy, and their role and function should be understood by all staff on entry to the school. The unit – or whatever you choose to call it – should provide separate short-term teaching and support programmes tailored to the needs of the individual disaffected pupil, whether this is anger management, social skills, or problem-solving. If the root of their problem is language based (as is so much behaviour), or if pupils do not have adequate basic skills, where are you meeting those needs? The Learning Support Unit can provide a safe part-time, temporary haven for pupils who have emotional difficulties or who have just arrived in school, perhaps as refugees with little English, while assessments are made and they learn school routines.

As an Inclusion Manager, you will need to have oversight of the Learning Support Unit. Day-to-day running should be done by an LSU manager who has training, experience and warm but firm relationships with pupils. All staff should have opportunities for further training and should be involved in training the mainstream staff in behaviour management techniques. Staff in the LSU need time for planning and curriculum development and should not just be reactive. All mainstream staff should be encouraged to visit and to be involved in the LSU curriculum so that pupils can reintegrate easily into mainstream. You as a member of the senior leadership team should review the work of the LSU annually and evaluate the provision. Is it reaching challenging targets in the Behaviour Support Plans? The bottom line is: 'What effect has it had on pupil achievement?' By that, I don't just mean academic standards but progress in personal development as well as academic progress compared to pupils' starting points. Lastly, if pupils are returned to a classroom which still does not meet their needs, can you get lasting improvement? Before reintegration, the LSU manager must work with teachers to adapt strategies to the returning pupil.

Sometimes the off-site, small-group, intimate environment of a Pupil Referral Unit (PRU), with the opportunity for a high degree of interaction with adults, suits some pupils who have difficulties in an ordinary mainstream school. This can be part-time and is usually accessed through your local authority. Again, they are meant as temporary provision. You will need to research in your own authority what links exist between the PRU and any outreach or behaviour support team.

Getting accreditation for your school

When your school is doing a good job, you want the pupils to benefit and go off with some qualification that acknowledges their work. You'll also want the rest of the world to acknowledge that you are a good school.

These are some qualifications at Key Stage 4.

Unit Award Scheme

The AQA exam board's Unit Award Scheme will accredit and certificate many unusual pieces of work as well as break up longer courses into manageable chunks. This is particularly apt if you are working with disaffected pupils or where attendance is interrupted – for example, pupil referral units and hospital schools – but there is no reason why you should not use the units in mainstream, as Tamarside Community College, Plymouth, do.

With AQA units (www.aqa.org.uk/qual/uas), you can recognise the achievement of students of all abilities in, for example, work-related learning and work experience, personal, social and health education, enrichment activities, citizenship, sport and outdoor pursuits:

*   Centres can write their own units.
*   Centres can use units written by other centres.

- Centres can use 14 AQA certificate-of-achievement courses and break them down into chunks. AQA provides a certificate for each part.
- Centres can use the units to provide interim accreditation.

GCSE Citizenship

It is possible to have short-course GCSE accreditation worth half a GCSE through AQA and Edexcel.

Certificate of Personal Effectiveness

Certificate of Personal Effectiveness (COPE), sometimes still known as Award Scheme Development and Accreditation Network (ASDAN), is awarded at a number of levels. There is a wide range of courses, some of them short. They motivate the hard-to-reach and can be used at Key Stage 3, 4 or 5. ASDAN courses come at lots of different levels, and there are some that would suit pupils with severe learning difficulties. Pupils build up a portfolio of evidence and this is externally assessed.

Teachers need appropriate training before you can use this course, but it is counted as a GCSE equivalent in your school's performance table returns to the DCSF. Again, this is a good way of giving awards for PSHE, citizenship, work-related learning, volunteering and key skills. Courses are practical and skill-based, and I have seen them used successfully in settings from special schools to academic sixth forms.

QCA 14–19 Diploma

Teaching is expected to begin for this in September 2009. This qualification will enable students to gain knowledge, understanding and hands-on experience of sectors that they are interested in, while putting new skills into practice. For example, as part of a Diploma in engineering, students could learn about how physics is applied in the workplace through a project in a local engineering company. Diplomas in business administration and finance, environmental and land-based studies, hair and beauty, hospitality, catering and manufacturing will be available from September 2009. The criteria for these are available from www.qca.org.uk.

Post-16 and transition

Education Maintenance Allowances are available for 16–19 year olds wanting to continue with full-time education. They can claim up to £30 per week (2008). Information is available at http://ema.direct.gov.uk/ema.html. There is an application pack and an information pack for parents that you might find useful to download and have available for parental interviews. On the same site, 'Care to learn' will pay young parents under 20 up to £160 (£175 in London) for registered childcare and travel costs if they want to continue with their education in a range of settings. Connexions Personal Advisors can help with more information.

Pupils with learning difficulties and disabilities often do not have a lot of choice when it comes to moving on from school, especially if they live in a rural area. An organisation called Skill – the national bureau for students with disabilities – provides information and advice on life beyond school, whether it is to employment, further education, higher education or training. It also covers benefits and tax, accessibility technology, and preparing to make decisions before leaving school. Their leaflets are available at www.skill.org.uk/info/infosheets.

Natspec, the National Association of Specialist Colleges for pupils with special needs, has a very useful website that not only lists specialist colleges, including their curriculum and support, but also has advice for parents on choosing a college. Their listings cover England and Wales and are organised by specialism. They are at www.natspec.org.uk.

Getting accreditation for your work on inclusion

Your school can be externally accredited for its work. The process as well as the outcome are beneficial to your school:

- It is an external validation of your practice.
- Going through the process of finding evidence and evaluating practice yourself makes you better informed as a manager.
- Areas for development are highlighted, and this can feed into your development plan.
- Staff are rewarded for their work and are motivated to keep up standards.

Basic Skills Quality Mark

There are two versions of Basic Skills Quality Mark: primary and secondary. The mark sets minimum standards for literacy and numeracy. It is awarded for three years, during which time the school is monitored to make sure standards don't slip. At the end of the three years, you can reapply. You are able to use the logo on your communications. Schools see it as a useful self-review and evaluation tool. The Basic Skills Agency accredits the local authority to assess your school. They are looking for:

- a whole-school strategy and action plan for basic skills;
- assessing need and monitoring and reviewing pupil progress;
- setting targets for improvement;
- a commitment to improving teaching skills in literacy and numeracy;
- using a range of teaching styles and materials to improve basic skills;
- informing and involving parents;
- monitoring the action plan and assessing improvement.

Further details are at www.quality-mark.org.uk.

British Dyslexia Association Quality Mark

This is awarded to local authorities and children's services that audit themselves and submit evidence. To see if your local authority is involved, go to www.bdadyslexia. org.uk/qmleas.html.

Inclusion Quality Mark

This is awarded to schools that can display evidence of reaching the standard across ten criteria. The school is assessed by a trained Inclusion Quality Mark (IQM) external assessor using a detailed framework that is tied in closely to Every Child Matters and mapped against the school's own Self-Evaluation Form. It is very thorough. Each item receives a grade of S, for securely in place; D, in place but needs development; or N, not yet in place.

The school's policy, awareness and practice are graded for each item. For example, 'Linked pastoral and behaviour policies' or 'Effective induction' each has three grades. You need to state where the assessor would find the evidence, but this can be referenced to sections in the Ofsted School Self-Evaluation Form (SEF). It is designed to be a hands-on working document that will change and develop with the needs of the school. Standards are rigorous, but everything need not be absolutely perfect yet for you to get the award. Further information from www.inclusionmark.co.uk.

NACE Challenge Award

If you want accreditation for your gifted and talented work, you could use the NACE (National Association for Able Children in Education) Challenge Award self-evaluation criteria at www.nace.co.uk. Schools that have systematically developed quality provision and action planning can apply for it.

Chapter 6

Monitoring the quality of learning

What constitutes progress?

Within the wide range of pupils with learning difficulties and disabilities, you will be looking for different types of progress. You probably have data on reading and spelling ages based on termly tests for those pupils who are having extra literacy help. With some pupils, you will be looking for progress in independence and social skills or behaviour. What is missing in many schools is guidance on what rate of progress is adequate.

'Special Educational Needs and Disability: Towards inclusive schools' (2004) suggests the following criteria for good progress for pupils with SEN in mainstream schools:

- At least 80 per cent of pupils make a gain of one level (either National Curriculum or P levels) at KS3.
- At least 34 per cent of pupils below level 2 in English in Year 7 gain one level by the end of KS3, and 55 per cent of pupils at level 2 gain one level by the end of KS3.
- Pupils withdrawn for substantial literacy support make an average of double the normal rate of progress. (A 'satisfactory rate of progress' is generally accepted as two sub-levels per year.)
- Attendance of pupils with special needs is above 92 per cent in secondary schools, and unauthorised absence is low.

The same report criticised the way progress is assessed by counting up the number of targets on the Individual Education Plan that had been achieved in a fixed period. What was effective was target setting within the curriculum based on thorough knowledge of the individual as part of a whole-school policy on assessment. The report also criticised the over-reliance on commercial packages for broad categories of pupils. More successful schools had more personalised programmes so there was suitable challenge for all pupils.

The Children's Plan of 2007 pointed to the need for a measure of progress of pupils with SEN in the light of greater personalised learning, and a report on this is due in 2009. At the time of writing, the Department for Children, Schools and Families (DCSF) and the National Strategies are together developing guidance on what constitutes progress for pupils with SEN/LDD including those below level 1. They are looking at practice across local authorities and planning to develop an equivalent point score for pupils working at P levels so that RAISEonline can include these pupils more effectively.

While the day-to-day testing and compilation of data may not be part of your role, you will need opportunities to challenge the rate of progress of individual pupils. There may be limited opportunity for extra withdrawal lessons. Most of the learning is going to take place in mainstream lessons. Some pupils with specific literacy needs are going to need extra, and they will need skilled interventions, planned in detail, if they are going to close the gap. As the astute Bart Simpson points out, 'remedial' classes are taught more slowly in order to help pupils catch up, which he rightly perceives as ironic. Bart's reading and spelling ages need to progress considerably faster than his chronological age.

Recording progress in personal development is less straightforward. Special schools have more experience of this. Pupils with behavioural, emotional and social difficulties can have behaviour logs and records of rewards, monitoring and meetings with pastoral staff. Some schools set personal targets such as helping at clubs, involvement in the community or being punctual, and these are checked out in tutor time once a week. A number have kept on an adaptation of the National Record of Achievement, putting the onus on pupils to log their own achievements in and out of school.

While the quality of the curriculum is important for pupils' engagement and progress, good individual assessment, and good teaching, with planning well matched to individual needs, are the major factors in raising achievement. A good assessment system would look like this:

*   Initial assessment of pupils' underperformance is early, rapid and accurate.
*   Pupils' progress is closely monitored and tracked across time and subjects.
*   Pupils are actively involved in setting their own targets and judging if they have met success criteria.
*   Test results and targets are shared with pupils and all staff involved in teaching them.
*   Pupil achievement is benchmarked against local and national data. This is an area that has been underdeveloped in SEN. Fischer Family Trust data give individual targets at different levels of aspiration, and you could use this as the basis of your target setting.
*   The results inform lesson planning and interventions by turning the data into words. For example, 'What is this pupil's next step in this curricular area?'
*   Parents are informed and involved to support pupils' achievements.

Inclusive schools set individual learning targets for all groups of pupils or individuals. Where this is the case, pupils with learning difficulties and disabilities will not usually require separate targets.

Does it matter where pupils are taught?

The Ofsted report from July 2006, 'Inclusion: Does it matter where pupils are taught?', came to the conclusion that there was effective provision for pupils with learning difficulties and disabilities in both special and mainstream schools, but more good or outstanding provision existed in resourced mainstream schools. By this they meant schools that had a 'unit' or 'designated special provision' where pupils spent some of their time, with the rest of their time spent in mainstream class for academic reasons, not just social. Pupils benefited academically, personally (increasing independence and ability to organise themselves) and socially (pupils' relationships and behaviour in a variety of situations). This includes pupils with profound and multiple learning difficulties and severe learning difficulties, including behaviour. It was not a case of additional resources making the big difference, however:

- The involvement of a specialist teacher who had qualifications and experience across a range of learning difficulties and disabilities. Pupils made better academic progress than those who had support from classroom assistants.
- Good assessment.
- Work tailored to challenge pupils sufficiently.
- Commitment from school leaders to create opportunities to include all pupils and ensure good progress for all of them.

Where pupils were not making enough progress, this was because:

- Pupils with behavioural, emotional and social difficulties got support too late, and it was ineffective. The statementing process disadvantaged them because it determined the quantity of support rather than the quality.
- Schools did not evaluate the progress of pupils with learning difficulties and disabilities as rigorously as other pupils. It was therefore difficult to compare the effectiveness of different provision.
- There is not enough done to improve the achievement of pupils in the lowest 25 per cent (in terms of Average Points Score).
- There was still not enough multi-agency work going on.

The report recommends that schools should 'improve the progress of pupils with learning difficulties and disabilities by using pupil level data that is relevant to their age and starting point to ensure they are suitably challenged'. This is rather vague. Dr Michael Farrell, in *The Special Education Handbook* (2009: 225), offers a solution to evaluating how much progress is enough for pupils with special needs. He says:

> One approach is to try to evaluate the progress made by special children in relation to that expected of children without a disability or disorder. By definition a special child has a disability or disorder and the disability or disorder makes education more difficult. Therefore, broadly, if a special child were to make the same progress as that expected for all children, or better, then this could presumably be considered excellent progress. Somewhere below such a level of progress, other judgements might be placed. For example, would less than half the progress expected of all children represent unsatisfactory progress? Would some point a little above such progress be seen as satisfactory? Would a point perhaps mid way between satisfactory and excellent progress constitute 'good' progress? Another factor that would be included would be the attainment level of the child in relation to his age. If a young person aged 16 years old with profound cognitive impairment were functioning on an assessment at a level typical of a child of one or two years old, expectations of, for example, 'satisfactory' progress would be likely to be much lower than half the progress of a typically developing individual. This is not to lower expectations randomly but to take account of the rate of progress already made in the student's development and bring this to bear on judgements of progress and expectations.

The government report adds that mainstream schools should:

- analyse critically their use and deployment of teaching assistants;
- increase the amount of specialist teaching provided for a range of LDD within a broad and balanced curriculum;
- develop knowledge and skills relating to learning difficulties and disabilities across the school workforce.

Special schools should:

- collaborate and share expertise more effectively to develop specialist teaching in mainstream schools.

So the main challenges for you as an Inclusion Manager are the questions:

Are pupils with BESD being picked up early enough?
How high are exclusions and internal seclusion? What is the trend? Does your school behaviour system enable early referral to a behaviour specialist who can set some interventions in place? How early do the learning mentors get involved, and how soon does the pupil get referred to a multi-agency meeting that might cast some light on the situation and provide some wider support? The evidence is that pupils with BESD are put on the SEN register too late, and until they are officially 'authenticated' as having a problem, they are more likely to be excluded.

How can you develop expertise across your staff in dealing with the range of learning difficulties and disabilities?
As I've written elsewhere, staff development is the key. Teachers might spend as little as a day of their initial training on learning difficulties and disabilities, yet a large proportion of your pupils may have LDD. Training needs to have a high profile in your school so that there are always questions at performance reviews based on pupil progress data, and this is linked to professional development as well as opportunities to share knowledge more informally.

Is classroom support deployed effectively? And how can you improve the quality?
Lesson observations by the senior management team and subject leaders need to focus on the quality of classroom support from time to time, but first staff need guidance on what constitutes effective classroom support. This guidance can also be in the staff handbook. Get support staff involved in monitoring progress, ask them whether they are deployed effectively and what could be improved. What is the level of their expertise, and what do they feel are their training needs? With new support staff, establish this from the beginning and match them with an experienced mentor. Are support staff involved in performance reviews? And are you prepared to take competency measures if necessary?

Have you set challenging targets for progress for pupils with LDD?
Refer to the criteria for good progress earlier in this section. How will you make all staff aware of them? How will you integrate this with the school's existing target-setting procedures?

Inclusive teaching and learning: what does it look like?

There is nothing here that differs fundamentally from good teaching.

- All staff are aware of the particular needs of pupils and understand practical ways of meeting those needs
- They establish what pupils know already.
- Learning objectives are clear to each pupil.
- Assessment is regular and thorough and is used to plan future work and help pupils understand how they can improve. This means asking questions not only of those pupils with hands up, and marking that shows how to improve in language that pupils understand. It may also mean giving clear descriptors in pupil-friendly language of the next level they are aiming at.
- Teachers have high expectations and know that to raise achievement these pupils will need good rather than satisfactory teaching.
- Provide guided work in a small group where necessary.
- Teachers set targets with pupils. Pupils know their targets and the levels they are working towards. Having level descriptors in the front of exercise books, where pupils highlight the things they can do, can be simple and motivating. It is important that pupils know how they can achieve these levels. Marking should show this, and pupils should be able to tell you.
- Plan a variety of tasks, including talking to others and aiming activities at different learning styles. Make learning objectives and success criteria clear, and adapt tasks so that every pupil can access the curriculum. This may involve giving wordbanks or a scaffold for longer writing.
- Arrange seating so that all pupils can see/hear and there is circulation space. (It's obvious but not always done!) Do not isolate pupils either by sitting them separately or cutting them off by placing a teaching assistant between them and the class. Discussion with another pupil helps them rehearse their answers. Make sure there is a 'talking partner' for each pupil.
- Give work in chunks so that it is not overwhelming.

ICT

Use suitable resources, including information and communication technology not just to make lessons interesting but to enable some pupils to record their ideas. Use ICT – not just interactive whiteboards as blackboards, but to open up the whole internet and get the class gripped from the beginning. Get pupils involved at the front of the class. Younger teachers have ICT as part of their training. One of the areas that barely gets a mention in initial teacher training is the use of technology by pupils with special educational needs, so I make no apology about going into operational detail about this. It can make the difference between pupils being present in the class and being included. For example, there are cheap word processors that work without waiting to boot up and do not have the 'fiddle factor' of laptops, but give reluctant writers with poor self-esteem the chance to make mistakes discretely. It's possible to add predictive text. Many dyslexic pupils can recognise a correct word but cannot spell it. Make sure there's a printer available in the classroom and a safe place to store the laptop during PE and lunchtime, and possibly a trusty, altruistic friend or TA to carry it from class to class. Get parents to sign an indemnity form if the word processor goes home. A comprehensive source of assistive technology is at www.inclusive.co.uk. Within your area there will be advisors in assistive technology attached to your local authority or an organisation such as CENMAC (www.cenmac.com) or one of the ACE centres (www.ace-centre.org.uk) in your region. There is a national list of these advisory services on the Becta website, with links to the various organisations at http://schools.becta.org.uk/index.php?section=tl& catcode=ss_tl_inc_ac_03&rid=13431.

The Inclusive Technology website also offers consultancy and training. Getting a consultant in is particularly useful if you have pupils with severe or complex needs who may need not just an alternative way of accessing a computer but communication equipment too. Some of the organisations on the Becta list – those staffed by teachers with an expertise in educational technology – offer suggestions for teaching and the curriculum as well as hardware and software. Another good source of support and advice is the SENIT discussion forum, where you may find the wheel has already been invented and adapted (www.communities.becta.org.uk/inclusion/senit).

The Inclusion Development Project was launched in October 2007 and will last for four years. It has developed resources and interactive DVDs for high-incidence special educational needs in mainstream schools and Early Years settings. Each year will have a different focus: first, dyslexia, speech, language and communication needs; then, autistic spectrum disorders (ASDs) and behavioural and emotional difficulties; and lastly, moderate learning difficulties. At the time of writing, there is no direct web link, but details will be on the DCSF website.

Lessons out of class

Withdrawal lessons for appropriate interventions are not meant to be an alternative curriculum. They should be time limited – say, for eight weeks – and have very clear targets. If that particular intervention has not worked, then why do more of the same? To state the obvious, pupils need to make reading gains of one year in a year just to keep in the same place. To catch up they need to make outstanding progress. Although it was done in 2002, there is research on the comparative effectiveness of literacy interventions. It should be treated with caution because there were other variables, and it is not certain if reporting was always accurate. However, it gives some pointers towards choosing a scheme. It is at www.dfes.gov.uk/research/data.uploadfiles/RR380.pdf.

If you haven't already, you will need to set up a reporting system so that you can share information with all staff on the progress of 'included' groups and pupils. Subject leaders will need to take responsibility for adapting schemes of work and for monitoring the quality of learning in their subject. The opportunity to do a dual lesson observation with you will help to standardise what learning experience you are expecting to see.

What to look for in lessons

You need to check that everything you want to happen is happening. All lesson observations in the school would benefit from having an emphasis on looking at learning rather than teaching, and by having a specific focus. Examples might be:

- Looking at a particular group – high achievers, pupils at School Action, EAL pupils. How fully are they involved, or how much progress do they make?

- Looking at the quality of support for statemented pupils with and without a teaching assistant.
- Asking how successful is assessment/marking/plenary/behaviour management?

Other evidence about the quality of learning might come from book trawls where you and colleagues compare the same group's exercise books from different subjects, or from 'Learning Walks' where you spend 10–15 minutes in each of a series of classrooms looking at a particular aspect of learning.

Where to start: an example

This should lead on from your analysis of data (see Chapter 2, How well is your school doing?), where you were able to pick out some classes or subjects in which a particular group of pupils were not doing as well as others. An example might be EAL pupils' writing in Year 9. Although pupils pick up conversational English quickly, researchers say that it takes between five and seven years to have an equal grasp of academic written English. Alternatively, pick out a lesson where pupils with LDD are doing exceptionally well and find out why.

Arrange with teachers to observe some lessons so that you see a variety of writing demands, not just in English lessons, but perhaps science and the humanities as well. You could go in unannounced, but since you have limited opportunities for observing, use it as a professional development experience and at least tell the teacher what you expect to find in the lesson plan.

You will need a lesson plan that identifies the different groups in class and some information about pupils' English language levels, what extra support they have, and what information and strategies the class teacher has been given already. Instead of looking at 'teaching', make your focus 'learning' and the factors that make that learning outstanding, good, satisfactory or inadequate.

Write 'How does the standard of writing of EAL pupils compare with others in Year 9 science?' at the top of your observation sheet. Look at pupils' books, both EAL and non-EAL. Look for common difficulties that EAL pupils may have over time, and how the teacher's marking is helping them to improve. What are the writing demands of this lesson? What strategies is the teacher using in this lesson that are helping these pupils fine tune their written English? Is there sufficient visual support for the spoken language – new vocabulary on the wall, for example? Is there enough opportunity for pupils to learn from each other? Does the plenary involve these pupils? What progress does the teacher feel they are making? Talk to more fluent pupils about their entry to your school (at another time if necessary, but feed this back to staff). What was useful in starting to learn English? Who do they think was most influential in teaching them – specialist staff, subject teachers, pupils? How effective do they feel teachers' marking is? Can they describe a really helpful lesson and suggest why it was? Look at the teacher's records to see how EAL pupils are progressing and what standards they are reaching. Are they finding some aspects of the work more difficult than others?

Feed back to the class teacher sensitively, saying what you felt was helpful and making one suggestion that would enable EAL pupils to learn faster and reach higher standards.

Add any other observations on EAL teaching generally from support staff. This information can be fed back to middle managers without naming the teachers, but along the lines of 'this worked, this did not work so well', with the express expectation that it will be passed on to colleagues in their subject area. For example, the observation that problem-solving in groups can be very successful. It can also become part of the staff handbook/induction pack with teaching suggestions. Alternatively, you might like it to be part of an INSET day or staff meeting. Where there is regular training in EAL and it is part of the School Improvement Plan involving a range of staff in the school, teachers are more likely to include EAL pedagogy in their practice.

Lesson observation: learning checklist

Some people like tick lists. To focus on learning in different groups will mean that you will need a range of evidence during the lesson: planning, pupils' comments, their books, interactions between the teacher and pupils, assessment. You could use the following checklist alongside supplementary notes to illustrate your feedback:

Table 6.1 Lesson observation: learning checklist

Focus of observation: is teaching inclusive?	✓ or ✗
Do pupils understand the purpose of the lesson?	
Does the teacher make connections with earlier learning/other subjects?	
Does planning show an understanding of the particular needs of individuals/groups (IEPs, statements, etc.)?	
Does the seating plan maximise learning?	
Is everyone's learning checked as the lesson develops?	
Does questioning draw in a cross-section of pupils?	
Do pupils' books show regular helpful marking?	
Do pupils know what to do to improve?	
Do books show a variety of ways of recording?	
Do activities allow all the pupils to make some progress?	
Does the lesson engage all pupils? Is it fun/interesting/challenging?	
Are staff expectations high enough? What evidence do you have for this?	
Does the teacher communicate clearly?	
Is the role of support staff always effective?	
Is the behaviour management policy of the school followed?	
Do support staff record progress and report back to the teacher?	
Is there enough plenary time to sum up and check on learning?	

Feedback dialogue

*   Who made most progress and why?
*   Who made least progress and why?

From Ann Sydney (2010) *A Handbook for Inclusion Managers*, London: Routledge. © 2010 Ann Sydney.

- What ideas do the teacher and support staff have to improve learning?
- What are your suggestions?
- When will you be back to see these being tried out?
- (If required) How would this lesson be graded according to the Ofsted framework? (Study the descriptors together.)

Suggestions for changes to improve a lesson

- Language: adapt, simplify, illustrate. Use wordbanks and visual aids such as mindmaps.
- Link assessment criteria to pupils' targets.
- Build on learning from other lessons.
- Talk about how they are learning, and model the activity first.
- Make learning objectives visible, and reiterate. (This doesn't mean the pupils have to spend half the lesson copying them from the board.)
- Modify tasks and resources.
- Deploy teaching assistants to groups to model/scaffold learning.
- Focus on oracy especially for EAL pupils: talk partners, hot seating, interviews.
- Use Bloom's taxonomy to frame different levels of questions.
- Vary teaching to match pupils' different learning styles.
- Vary grouping and seating to match the activity and improve behaviour.
- Use Assessment for Learning, and also use the teaching assistant to observe progress.
- Consider extra time before or after a lesson ('homework club'?) to prepare/consolidate learning, either 1:1 or small group.

Reviewing the progress of statemented pupils

All pupils with statements should have annual reviews. There is guidance on how to prepare and conduct these in the SEN Toolkit (DCSF 2001). Reviews are usually attended by a representative of the local authority who is there to judge whether the statement should be continued in the light of current progress. The school needs to provide information on progress against the targets in the statement. The pupil should attend, but they may need an advocate or training beforehand in what is required of them in an annual review, to give them confidence to give their own opinions. It is very easy for well-meaning adults to hijack the process. Parents/carers, with advocates if necessary, and representatives from other involved agencies should be there. Some schools block all their reviews at the same time of year rather than the anniversary of the statement. Unfortunately, this tends to be at the end of the summer term when there is no continuity with the same subject staff being able to respond to the results of the review.

In Year 9 and following years, pupils have a Transitional Review (or '14+'). This is extremely important for statemented pupils because it will be the basis of planning for their wider future. A representative from social services and a specialist Connexions adviser who knows about provision for young adults with special needs should be present. Think hard about going ahead if they are not present because this review should cover the whole range of need – the curriculum at Key Stage 4, work experience and work-related learning, training or education at 16+, grants and housing if necessary. Pupils with cognitive difficulties often find it hard to look ahead. Expecting them to do this in the atmosphere of a review is unrealistic, and they will need preparation. As in other annual reviews, targets will be set for the coming year. The Transition Plan should indicate who is responsible for implementing the recommendations. However, the plan does not have the legal status of the statement: it is not legally enforceable. The same range of professionals should be present at Year 10 and 11 reviews. Pupils transfer to adult services at 16, and there should be preparation for this ahead of time. Sometimes the school and parents disagree about recommendations in the statement review, and dissenting views should be recorded. If parents disagree with the prevailing view, then they should (be helped to) write to the local authority as soon as possible.

Looked-after children have Personal Education Plans. The reviews are arranged annually by the 'looking after' local authority, and usually, but not always, take place in school. PEPs should include some background history, the pupil's strengths and weaknesses in school, any difficulties, updated progress, their interests and hobbies, attendance and punctuality and any concerns identified. The school has a responsibility to check on any absence on the first day and to provide catch-up classes.

Chapter 7

Working with others

Working with others will include a range of other agencies, other schools and educational settings, but a large part of your job is about working with pupils, parents and teachers.

Working with pupils

Given the opportunity, pupils will tell you if things are working. Most schools have a routine questionnaire loosely based on Every Child Matters, and they have a School Council. However, school councils can be unrepresentative and rarely get beyond discussing the state of the toilets, dinners and fund-raising. All very fundamental, but when do your pupils have the chance to discuss the curriculum or teaching and learning? Is the whole range of pupils represented? Representatives are invariably confident volunteers who have been elected by their class. You could bring together a cross-section of pupils informally to discuss particular issues such as bullying, what makes effective provision for pupils with literacy difficulties, or an aspect of equality. Effective schools do this.

At an individual level, pupils should help in decision making about their provision, but they do need guidance. The sequence should move from dependence on a teacher or teaching assistant, through modelling and shared/guided group activities, to independent work.

Working with parents and carers

What do your parents and carers want from your school? You will find life easier working with pupils if parents see themselves as partners. Does your school have a routine questionnaire that goes out? And if so, what information can you draw from it that relates to your work as Inclusion Manager? What is the most effective way to communicate with your parents? Are they consulted on whole-school issues as well as on matters related to their own child? Are they welcomed and involved in school activities rather than just summoned when there is a problem? Can you involve them by providing classes in literacy, English or how to deal with difficult behaviour? Some schools have a Parent Council similar to the School Council but with a role that is separate from Parent Governor.

Sometimes it is necessary or helpful to have a mediator between parents and the school – during the statementing process, for example, or around exclusion. Most local authorities have a Parent Partnership Officer who can do this. There was a successful 2007 pilot of Parent Support Advisers based in school, and the Steer Report of 2008 recommended more funding for this. Parent Support Advisers work with families not just on problems in school but also on those aspects of social deprivation that underpin pupils' performance such as housing and benefits.

If you do not fulfil your legal obligations for pupils with special educational needs and disabilities, parents can take your school and the local authority to SENDIST (the special educational needs and disability tribunal). Should this happen, you will need to have good records of provision, reviews and meetings with parents and other professionals. The tribunal provides guidance on procedures to the school and local authority before the case appears before it.

Working with staff

As an Inclusion Manager you are probably already experienced at managing change. You will know that successful change happens when teachers are the main agents of change and the pupils are the main focus of it. Successful change depends on what teachers do and think. All the research confirms that you cannot have lasting improvement if it is imposed from above without the ownership of the school staff. There is a lot of legislation that is imposed from above, and one of your many roles will be to interpret this and make it part of your school's systems by showing how it can benefit teachers and pupils. Teamwork, shared leadership and professional working relationships are what we are aiming for. The key is to keep teachers learning. Most teachers are teachers because they enjoyed learning when they were at school. Get them involved in sharing their expertise, whether this is in a faculty meeting where teachers and assistants share a way of observing behaviour or an approach to spelling; a demonstration to the whole staff of how ICT can benefit a pupil with dyslexia; or a departmental head explaining a new approach to raising achievement for gifted and talented pupils. On an individual level, perhaps newly qualified teachers (NQTs) or staff struggling with teaching pupils with EAL in their class could watch a lesson taught by an experienced practitioner. I have always felt that staff development is the key to change and school improvement. To get everyone committed, innovations have to improve the teacher's experience in the classroom and improve learning.

To ensure that change goes beyond writing a new policy and filing it, and that it actually has an impact on pupils' learning, there are certain well-worn criteria for success. Have these in mind when you are developing policies.

- Staff need to be willing to work on whole-school improvements.
- The focus for the planned changes should be pupils' learning – their progress and achievement.
- Leadership should be shared among a number of teachers.
- Every member of staff should have some piece of the action – specific responsibility for part of the plan.
- Staff training is linked to the changes.
- There are strategies for monitoring and evaluating the impact of the policy or plan.
- You will have considered what data you will need to establish further priorities.

This hopefully gets away from change being something that the senior management team do to the staff in response to a government initiative. There are often lots of simultaneous initiatives, and you need to focus on one at a time. Treat it like rock climbing. Too much change at the same time and you could end up falling off. You need to keep three points in contact with the rock-face while you move one.

Pupils are the focus of your work. Earlier I have written about listening to pupils and surveying their opinions. There are a number of companies that will survey parents or pupils for you if you prefer. This gives you the first stage in your school improvement cycle – the data. However, this leaves someone else – you? – to act on the data. If you involve pupils and teachers together as researchers and decision-makers, following through to action and a review of what needs to be done next, you are more likely to get a realistic view of what is happening in your school, and an improvement. You could apply this to homework, lunchtimes, after-school clubs, the sixth form PSHE curriculum and more. Follow this up to see if your efforts have made a difference to pupils' everyday experience.

One of the difficult tasks for an Inclusion Manager is ensuring that referrals for behaviour are made early enough. Some teachers see a referral as a sign of weakness, a criticism of their classroom management skills, even when this is not the case, and they wait for another teacher to refer. To get around this, open up referrals so that anyone can refer, and encourage classroom assistants to do this. They are also more likely to see the behaviour happening in different classes. Ensure your teaching assistants have training in observing and recording behaviour, and this can provide valuable information to plan interventions and objective evidence.

Working with special schools

In 2003, the DfES reviewed the role of special schools and recommended that they become more outward-looking centres of excellence, providing outreach for mainstream schools. With medical advances, the population of pupils with severe and complex needs is growing, and special schools increasingly care for these pupils, in close collaboration with health and social services. All local authorities have at least one special school. Many are generic, while some have a specialism. A small number are residential. They are a great source of expertise and specialist resources, and have often developed innovative curricula. One of your many challenges as Inclusion Manager is to develop your staff's skills. One way of doing this is to buy in expertise either as support or training under a Service Level Agreement with a special school.

In the Service Level Agreement, you should produce a document saying what will be provided by each school, over what period, who is responsible for this, and how it will be paid for. It should include a date for review and should be signed by the headteacher in each school.

The 2006 Ofsted report 'Inclusion: Does it matter where pupils are taught?' found that there was little evidence of special and mainstream schools working well together, even when they were co-located. For some time now, some statemented pupils have been able to experience other settings through dual placements. Most of this inclusion movement is from special school to mainstream and can be part-time, full-time, temporary or permanent. Not all pupils want or need to be included all of the time. Typically, inclusion would be for 51 per cent of the week, and the pupil would be on the roll of the mainstream school. Occasionally pupils travel in the other direction when their needs change – for example, to a Pupil Referral Unit or special school. Unfortunately PRUs are not always seen as part of the continuum of provision but as somewhere pupils go only if they are excluded. Part-time placements at PRUs can be very effective in preventing exclusion, especially if PRU staff train mainstream staff and support them with reintegration. Many special schools now have outreach teams that do a similar job.

If your school is one where transfer of statemented pupils hasn't yet happened, then take time to prepare the ground, because failure will affect not just those pupils who you are currently working with. It is important to get the systems right. Especially useful further reading is *Closing the Inclusion Gap*, by Rita Cheminais (see Further reading). Some local authorities provide their own guidance, including how pupils are identified.

There are various models of working with special schools, ranging from a hard federation to the inclusion of a group of pupils at extra-curricular events. With groups, you might share inclusion projects such as environmental awareness, perhaps as part of an ASDAN course. You could have classes visiting each other or pupils coming in for special curriculum events such as Arts Week. Your pupils could act as supporters and tutors for sports activities. Your staff might share staff meetings or training, or you could swap staff and resources. Individual pupils or classes could come to your school for part of their timetable.

The first thing you need to be clear about is why you are doing any of these, and the answer should be to further the pupils' academic and/or personal achievement. You need to start by making contact with the special school (if they haven't approached you already) and testing the water. They may already have identified pupils who need the academic boost or social experience of a mainstream placement. Your local education officer (SEN) will probably be a mine of information. Raising awareness of inclusion in your own school is the next step. Start with the senior management team because it won't happen longer term if you don't have their backing. Get them to promote the idea, while you work on the staffroom. Even the nicest people in the staffroom can find health and safety reasons why they should not have extra pupils included in their classes. You will need to do some staff training on the legal background, perhaps some role-play if this hasn't been overdone already, and give some indication of the strengths and weaknesses of pupils you might include. Pick some pioneering staff who are keen for inclusion to succeed. They should be encouraged to visit the special school, talk to teachers and join in with classes there as part of the preparation.

Identify your counterpart in the special school. Use both school timetables and the special school's knowledge of their pupils to establish who would benefit and when the placement will take place. Involve teachers in your own school and support staff from the special school in planning from the start so they feel some ownership. Get parents' views and written consent early on. Setting up inclusion is time consuming, but after the first time, it gets easier. Keep the senior leadership team in both schools and your staff informed of all your actions.

There are a number of things that conspire to torpedo successful inclusion, and you need to get these sorted out early in the process:

- transport arrangements;
- support staff who do not want to work in mainstream;
- disagreements over who provides/pays for specialist resources;

- uncertainty over who assesses progress and sets targets (especially if pupils are working at P levels);
- timetables that clash so that the pupil misses out on important parts of the curriculum or therapy.

It helps if you can think these through and talk to your local authority SEN officer. Draw up an agreement before any pupil moves anywhere, clarifying responsibilities and the roles of staff involved. Both headteachers could sign it. Keep notes on everything you do. Have the school's health and safety representative write risk assessments and suggest improvements.

You will need to gather information on pupils who can travel backwards and forwards between sites with them. Many special schools now have a Pupil Passport (see Sally Millar's work at the CALL Centre) detailing their needs, likes and dislikes, and giving tips to helpers so that there is more social interaction. You may need to have information on communication and how the pupil uses ICT. Statements, Individual Education Plans and targets should all be in the file as well as emergency contact numbers, notes on toileting if necessary, how to handle behaviour and the procedure in case of fire. A contact book is essential. It makes sense for a teaching assistant to come from the special school who knows the pupil and their routines well, perhaps for an agreed fixed period. It is really important that this person is welcomed by the staff because they are pivotal to the success of the inclusion. They will need to be introduced to the mainstream school's routines and expectations, as well as its policies, especially Child Protection and the Behaviour and Inclusion policies. You need to have back-up systems if the teaching assistant is absent or unable to meet any specialised transport. It is useful if one of your teaching assistants shadows initially so that they can exchange information and your school's TA learns what is involved.

Inclusion will have an impact not just on the pupils coming into mainstream but on class teachers and other pupils as well. Prepare them for it and collect their opinions once it is happening. This will help you deal with any problems and improve practice.

Keep clear records of what you do and how the pupils are progressing so that you can evaluate the success of the inclusion. Ensure the included pupils are part of your school's assessment and pastoral system. They are not visitors.

Once they are up and running, the inclusion arrangements need to be evaluated. This should involve parents, the pupil, special school staff, the teaching assistant, class teachers in your school and the tutor. It would be useful if the local education officer (SEN) could attend, as they can often contribute their experience.

- Is the pupil happy with this new arrangement? What could be better?
- Is the pupil getting a broad and balanced curriculum?
- Are they making progress academically and socially?
- Are they getting the same range of therapies as similar special-school pupils?
- Are there any extra resources needed?
- Are there any health and safety issues?

Working with Regional Partnerships

There are ten Regional Partnerships sponsored by the DCSF. They bring together children's services across a region to promote inclusion and positive outcomes for children with special educational needs and/or disabilities and looked-after children. Typically they would decide their own priorities, which might be training or setting up regional provision for low-incidence special needs. The Regional Partnerships provide a useful mediation service between, for example, parents and schools.

Provision for gifted and talented pupils is organised by the Regional Partnerships, with Excellence hubs – centres of higher education in each region – providing extra-curricular activities. The website http://ygt.dcsf.gov.uk also has useful guidance for identifying gifted and talented pupils in your school and gives contact details for your regional hub.

The South West Regional Partnership has produced a very useful handbook on setting up links between special and mainstream schools. It includes examples of service level agreements, describes a range of good practice, and gives information on funding and advice on identifying suitable link staff.

Working with other agencies

You will need the expertise of people outside your field. External agencies and teams can provide you with resources, expertise and information that you would not normally have. In return, they are accountable to you for results. Do you have a service level agreement with outside agencies that clarifies what each side expects and what is included in the cost?

Depending on where you work, there could be many or few agencies to work with. Some teams, such as the Behaviour and Education Support Teams, are multi-disciplinary and work on attendance as well as behaviour. You may choose to have a Safer School Partnership Officer, a police officer who can help you with school safety and crime prevention. Some specialist and valuable services, such as speech and language therapy, can be thin on the ground. Others may have lots of temporary staff. All have a history of different ways of working and a different vocabulary and jargon. None of this is insurmountable if you focus on outcomes. What you have in common is the welfare and achievement of the child. Regular multi-agency meetings give opportunities to share information, and many schools have set up their own internal Inclusion Panels to ensure the right provision is in place. When you are working with other agencies, it is important to keep records of agreed outcomes. You need to present information positively but honestly while avoiding jargon. Be clear about what each side is capable of doing and who is accountable for action.

Since it is unlikely you will have ongoing support from other agencies, external therapists should be encouraged to leave behind programmes and interventions to support pupils and, if necessary, train staff in how to implement them.

Working with other agencies is at the heart of Every Child Matters. From April 2006, every local authority has had a Children and Young People Plan that brings together all local authority planning for children and young people. Look at your local authority's website for details of this. Local authorities have developed information-sharing databases into which education, social services and health put in key information about vulnerable children. Each local authority has an Information Sharing and Assessment Team which is a central source of information for everyone involved in inclusion. An important part of this new way of working is the Common Assessment Framework.

The Common Assessment Framework

The Common Assessment Framework was to be implemented everywhere by the end of 2008. It is designed to be used at an early stage, before serious problems arise, and should mean that a child is assessed only once. A teacher I know with cerebral palsy said that his childhood was one long stream of pleasant people, whom he only knew by first name, asking him the same questions and wasting his time. The CAF should also help standardise language and protocols; any teacher who has been in a multi-agency meeting chaired by a professional from a different service may recognise the need for this.

The following is based on information at www.dfes/commoncore/docs/CAFQuick Guide.doc.

You can do a common assessment at any time when you are concerned about how well a child (or unborn baby) or young person is progressing. You might be concerned about their health, welfare, behaviour, progress in learning or any other aspect of their well-being. It may be that their needs are unclear, or broader than your school can address; and a common assessment would help identify the needs, and/or get other services to help meet them. The guidance says a child could have additional needs including or combining:

- disruptive or anti-social behaviour;
- overt parental conflict or lack of parental support/boundaries;
- involvement in or risk of offending;
- poor attendance or exclusion from school;
- experience with bullying;
- special educational needs;
- disabilities;
- disengagement from education, training or employment post-16;
- poor nutrition;
- ill-health;
- substance misuse;
- anxiety or depression;
- housing issues;
- pregnancy and parenthood.

Or they could have complex needs such as:

- children who are the subject of a child-protection plan;
- looked-after children;
- care leavers;
- children for whom adoption is the plan;
- children with severe and complex special educational needs;
- children with complex disabilities or complex health needs;
- children diagnosed with significant mental health problems;
- young offenders involved with youth justice services (community and custodial).

You do not need to do a common assessment where you have identified the needs and your school can meet them, or where you know how to get the required help from another service using established procedures. It does not replace the statementing procedure, but it could be used beforehand or in conjunction to get a broader picture of the child's needs. If you are unsure whether or not a child has already been referred by another agency, especially if they are new to your school, ring the Information Sharing number in your local authority. Eventually there is intended to be a national number that should more effectively pick up mobile families.

There is a checklist to help you decide whether a common assessment should be completed. It is designed to be used alongside existing assessments of a pupil – for example, as part of an Individual Education Plan/Pastoral Support Plan (IEP/PSP) review. Whether to do the assessment is a decision you should make jointly with the child and/or parent/carer. The pupil should be the person to decide with you, so long as they are old enough and competent to understand. Always encourage them to discuss things with their parents/carers.

How to do a common assessment

Preparation

You talk to the child/young person and their parent. Explain that the Common Assessment Framework is a means of getting extra resources. You discuss the issues and what you can do to help. You talk to anyone else you need to – your manager, colleagues, other staff – including those in other agencies who are already involved with the child. You might also use the checklist. You decide if a common assessment would be useful and you seek the agreement of the child/young person and their parent as appropriate.

Discussion

You talk to the child, parent or family and complete the assessment with them. Focus on the whole child not just education. You make use of information you have already gathered from the child, family or other practitioners so they don't have to repeat themselves. If there is already a common assessment, you add to or update it with the family. At the end of the discussion, you hope to understand better the child's and family's strengths and needs, and what can be done to help. You agree on actions that your service and the family can deliver. You agree with the family on any actions that require others to deliver. You record this on the form.

Service delivery

You deliver on your actions. You make referrals or broker access to other services, using the common assessment to demonstrate evidence of need. Some agencies are reluctant, because of the nature of their work, to share information. It is still early days for CAF, and trust has to be built up between services. As Inclusion Manager, you need to establish protocols for working with other agencies and give them an understanding of how schools work. Some local authorities organise back-to-back assessments by different agencies, with the opportunity to observe the interaction behind a two-way mirror. Where the child or family needs services from a range of agencies, there should be a process across agencies to identify a lead professional. Commonly, by default, this is the person who chairs the first multi-agency meeting – often the SENCO – but it need not be.

You need to record what will happen next and record the family's agreement. The Ofsted report 'Inclusion: Does it matter where pupils are taught?' (2006) stresses that CAFs should focus on outcomes rather than provision. You will give the parents/carers a copy of the CAF. If consent to do a common assessment is refused, you can still share the information you have gathered, but you will need to consider carefully whether, for example, the public's/child's interest in sharing the information overrides the lack of consent. It may be the discussions have resolved any concerns and nothing needs to be done. The CAF does not guarantee action because this is unfortunately dependent on budgets. If needs are not met, take this up initially with your local authority or SEN Regional Partnership.

Download a copy of the form and guidance notes from www.everychildmatters. gov.uk/deliveringservices/caf.

Looked-after children

The latest figures available, for 2006, show that 60,300 children were in local authority care, spread among the 150 local authorities (Department for Education and Skills/National Statistics, 2007). The chances are some of them will be in your school. What do you know about them? Seventy per cent of these pupils are in foster care, while there are 3,200 unaccompanied asylum-seeking children. Looked-after children have poor attendance, underachieve by a long way and tend to drop out of education. These are the things you need to be monitoring and taking action on. To improve the life-chances of looked-after children, the government set out, in the report 'Care Matters: Time for change', ways of providing more stability and raising aspirations. One of the contributing pieces of research was on best practice in schools, researched during 2006. This is how the findings may affect you as a manager:

- A 'virtual headteacher' will look after the welfare of looked-after children.
- Free school transport will bring stability when fostering arrangements change.
- Popular schools, even if over-subscribed, will have to take on looked-after children.
- Schools will have to provide catch-up support to ensure looked-after children do not fall behind their classmates.

It is unlikely you will have many looked-after children. In the few schools that do, a member of staff usually has this overall responsibility, has the time and administrative support to do it, and the system works well. Local authorities have money under the Vulnerable Children Grant to set up extra help, but this money is not devolved to schools. Each local authority has a named person who co-ordinates provision. You can get the name of yours from the website at www.dfes.gov.uk/educationprotects, which is the central point for information on looked-after children. It is also where you will find a report on dealing with mobility generally. This is at www.educationprotects// upload/ACF1796.pdf.

An HMI report on 'Looked-After Children' was published in autumn 2007. It is part of a series of mini leaflets that will be produced on the theme of 'personalisation and diversity'.

Gypsy, Roma and traveller pupils

Because of their transient lifestyle, there are often significant interruptions to the education of Gypsy, Roma and traveller pupils. The average attendance among these groups is 75 per cent, the lowest of any ethnic group (Ofsted, 'Provision and Support for Traveller Pupils,' 5). Although these pupils make satisfactory or good progress in lessons, it is sustaining that progress that is the problem. They are the lowest achieving of all minorities, with girls outperforming boys.

Gypsy, Roma and travellers are recognised as distinctive groups. Some are housed or permanently settled but still identify as part of these communities; others, such as showmen and circus families, are very mobile and may only be settled in the winter. In particular, many of the families are mobile in September at the start of the school year, and transition between primary and secondary schools can be problematic.

In England and Ireland, Gypsies are recognised as a minority ethnic with a distinctive culture under the Race Relations Act. Your local authority should have a traveller education service to provide advice, advocacy for families, extra teaching and possibly a specialist Education Welfare Officer. Your aim should be to work in partnership with the service rather than being dependent on them. A clear service level agreement is a good start. Other schools in your area may have good practice and resources to pass on.

There are a number of issues that need to be addressed:

- Sharing information. Some families do not want to be identified as Gypsy, Roma or travellers, and you need to have respect for their sensitivities.
- Many of these children drop out after primary school, as many of their parents may have done. Only 60 per cent are enrolled at Key Stage 3, and less than 50 per cent at Key Stage 4. Literacy levels in families are sometimes low, so care must be taken in any communication with home.
- Information about previous schooling and the transfer of records. Phone calls to the Inclusion Manager or pastoral head and SENCO are often more effective than waiting for bureaucracy to grind on.
- Pupils changing schools often will not have the correct uniform. How big a barrier are you making this? Are there discreet ways of getting round it?
- Name-calling and bullying are often directed at these children, and this in turn leads to increased absence. Look at the whole-school ethos and the values your school is promoting. Is difference a threat or an opportunity? Does the personal and social education scheme of work refer to aspects of their culture and history?
- Staff often feel they lack information or resources to cope well and will need information and training. Perhaps Gypsies, Roma and travellers can be involved in this?
- How do you gather information about the day-to-day experience of these pupils in your school? Do Gypsy and traveller children and their families feel they are treated fairly? Are they included in your equality policies? As with other minority groups,

are you monitoring their achievement? When you have identified priorities for improvement, make sure these are in your inclusion strategy.

Working with other mainstream schools

You may be in a Federation, hard or soft, or part of an Excellence in Cities cluster and be used to working with other schools as part of everyday life. Even if you have no formal links yet, you might consider forging them to look at low-incidence SEN provision, or to standardise your approach to behaviour. Successful cluster arrangements I have seen have involved groups of schools buying in a speech and language therapist not just to work with individuals but also to be part of team teaching. In other cases, headteachers or Inclusion Managers have set up a panel with the local Pupil Referral Unit to look at exclusions. Other schools have used links to improve pupils' personal development and well-being (PDWB) by widening their horizons, whether this is through activities aimed at gifted and talented pupils or international links with developing countries. Another reason to link together is to make more opportunities for 'managed moves'. Your local authority will usually have a protocol to follow. The government recommended, in Sir Alan Steer's 2005 report, that secondary schools should be in behaviour partnerships to work together to improve behaviour, tackle persistent absence and improve outcomes for those whose behaviour is poor. Sir Alan's report recommended that participation in behaviour partnerships should be compulsory from 2008.

Chapter 8

Reporting to others

Governors

Governors have legal obligations to report to the local authority on special educational needs and vulnerable children, and to parents on what the school provides, but much of their information will come from you. As Inclusion Manager, you may be asked to serve on one of the committees. In any case, you should raise the profile of inclusion by giving a regular update on staffing, training, new developments and progress. Ask the Examinations Officer to pick out the results of those pupils on the SEN register or other groups, and show their contextual value added to give an indication of their achievement.

When you are providing the governors with information, you could bear in mind the following, taken from 'Special Educational Needs and Disability: Towards inclusive schools' (DfES 2004). It suggests these criteria for inclusion:

- The school monitors its admissions and exclusions and analyses the information, together with the local authority, in relation to placements in other schools.
- Pupils with disabilities whose parents request a place at the school are admitted wherever possible, and the school makes reasonable adjustments to include them in the life of the school.
- There is careful preparation of placements, covering the pupils with SEN, their peers in school, parents and staff, with careful attention to the availability of sufficient and suitable teaching and personal support.
- Trends over time in National Curriculum and other assessments are analysed in the context of available data about comparative performance, and are scrutinised.
- Pupils' work is regularly discussed, and the quality of teaching of pupils with SEN is regularly observed.
- Evaluation of the quality of the provision is linked to the information about the outcomes for pupils.
- Those responsible are held to account for the quality of the provision, and plans to improve the outcomes are implemented.
- The school integrates its systems and procedures for pupils with SEN (including arrangements for assessment, recording and reporting) into the overall arrangements for all pupils.
- Deliberate steps are taken to involve parents of pupils with SEN as fully as possible in decision making, keeping them well informed about their child's progress and giving them as much practical support as possible.

Are you able to report to governors on all of these areas?

So who else are you reporting your successes to? Does your website celebrate your successes? Do you include celebrations as well as information in the newsletter to parents?

Parents

The school prospectus

Each year the governing body must publish a school prospectus for prospective parents. Schools can choose to put in what they like except for obligatory content on special educational needs (which was previously in the governors' annual report to parents). The following is taken from the DfES 'A Guide to the Law for School Governors'. Changes can be tracked on the www.governornet.co.uk website. Check that your prospectus includes:

- arrangements for the admission of pupils with disabilities;
- details of steps to prevent disabled pupils being treated less favourably than other pupils;
- details of existing facilities to assist access to the school by pupils with disabilities;
- the accessibility plan (required under the Disability Discrimination Act 1995) covering future plans for increasing access to the school by pupils with disabilities;
- information about the implementation of the SEN policy and any changes to the policy during the last year.

The prospectus must be published at least six weeks before the final date by which parents are asked to apply for admission/express a preference, so you will need to have this ready around Christmas of the preceding year.

The school profile

This is a description of how well the school is doing and is generally done early in the spring term when you have validated data, but it can be done at any time of the year. Parents will read this. It is completed online annually. As Inclusion Manager, you will not have direct responsibility for this but you may contribute to each of the narrative sections that cover:

- What are your successes?
- What are you trying to improve?
- How have your results changed over time?
- How are you ensuring that every child gets teaching to match their individual needs?
- How do you ensure pupils are safe, healthy and well supported?
- What have you done in response to the last Ofsted report?
- How do you work with parents and the community?

Each section is meant to be 100–200 words.

Letters and emails to parents

Note that there is software to translate into 75 languages at www.babylon.com.

Be positive in your dealings with parents, and talk about their children's strengths as well as their difficulties. It helps if you can be flexible about meeting times. Consider that they might also have disabilities or learning difficulties and might have 'baggage' about their own schooldays. Remember that you speak in jargon that is familiar to you, but not necessarily to people outside the field of education. Think about the problems you would have if you had to get to your child's school for a similar meeting.

Not all homes have working computers, nor does everyone have access at work, but it can be helpful if parents are able to access their child's attendance and punctuality record online. The Steer Report of 2008 emphasised the importance of working closely with parents as a way of improving behaviour, and this could be a starting point in preventing truancy.

Pupils' records

Under the Education Regulations 2005, schools have to transfer a curricular record for each pupil when they change schools. The record should be updated annually. Since 2005, parents have had the legal right to access their child's educational record. This does not include information that a teacher would have for their own use. It does include any statement of SEN (parents should already have an updated copy of this), Personal Educational Plan for a looked-after pupil, details of behaviour, progress and family background. There is information that is exempted from disclosure to parents:

- information that might cause serous physical or mental harm to the child or some-one else;
- child-protection information where disclosure would not be in the best interests of the child;
- references;
- reports to court;
- information recorded during an examination;
- information that relates to another person or identifies another person.

It is a bit of a minefield, and I am not a lawyer. If you are in this position, please check the current legislation and refer it upwards. If you have any doubts about disclosure, the school can contact the DCSF or the Information Commissioner. You have 15 school days from receipt of a parent's written request to provide the information. If a pupil puts in a written request, you have 40 days! The guidance says that pupils should be allowed to see their statement of SEN unless disclosure could cause serious harm to the child. With any of this, make sure you know whether sensitive information is present.

Ofsted

Inspection judgements

Since the shorter Ofsted inspections and reports started in September 2005, the Inspection Judgements form is attached to the school's very brief report, and it shows the grades given for every aspect of the school's work. While you will have a part in the whole school's performance, there are several judgements that relate closely to your work as Inclusion Manager. Judgements are one of four grades: outstanding, good, satisfactory or inadequate. The Ofsted Evaluation Schedule gives descriptors for some of these, such as behaviour, but with others it is down to the inspector's professional judgement, based on what you are able to show her as evidence. In an inspection that lasts a maximum of two days, including writing the report on the second afternoon, consider what sort of evidence might be appropriate. Any documentary evidence is triangulated by talking to pupils and members of staff, by observing lessons and activities outside lessons, or by analysing data. Do you have data that show the progress of different groups? Are you able to put your hands on information about vulnerable pupils' needs, provision and progress? As a manager, can you show the impact of your initiatives? Although the inspection team will have had access to RAISEonline to provide historical data, the previous inspection report, the school's Self-Evaluation Form, and possibly other data on attainment, they will not finalise their judgements until the end of the inspection. They will all be looking for evidence of current achievement through records, books and lessons during the inspection.

These are the areas of inspection that your job relates to:

Overall effectiveness

- How effective, efficient and inclusive is the provision of education, integrated care and any extended services in meeting the needs of learners?
- How well does the school work in partnership with others to promote learners' well-being?

Achievement and standards

- How well do learners make progress, taking account of any significant variations between groups of learners?
- How well do learners with learning difficulties and disabilities make progress?
- The behaviour of learners.

The quality of provision

- How effective are teaching and learning in meeting the full range of learners' needs?
- How well do the curriculum and other activities meet the range of needs and interests of learners?
- How well are learners cared for, guided and supported?

Leadership and management

- How effectively do leaders and managers at all levels set clear direction leading to improvement, and promote high-quality care and education?

- How well is equality of opportunity promoted and discrimination tackled so that all learners achieve as well as they can?
- How well does the school promote community cohesion?

The whole inspection team will be involved in making these judgements about aspects of inclusion. There are descriptors on the Ofsted website which will help you judge your school's performance yourself. They are at the elusive www.Ofsted.gov.uk/assets/ internet_Content/Shared_Content/IIFD/Files/schoolsFramework/usingTheEvaluation Schedule.pdf.

It is very possible that an inspector will want to meet you. They will want to see that you are analysing data for different groups and will want some evidence of how well different groups progress. They may want to discuss a small sample of pupils from the SEN register/EAL list/looked-after children with a range of needs to see what the school is providing and how good the links are with other agencies. Individual plans for pupils should be available as well as any statements and reviews. The conversation around these files gives lots of information for judgements, but it necessarily has to be short. However, the focus of each inspection is different, and you will not necessarily know if you are going to be seen until the timetable is fixed, possibly on the first morning of the inspection.

Inspectors will also be visiting classes with a definite focus for their lesson observations. This will depend on the issues identified in the Pre-Inspection Briefing written by the lead inspector and shared with the headteacher. The head generally shares the contents with the senior leadership team. One possible issue might be the underachievement of certain groups identified from the RAISEonline data. The inspectors might want to see how class teachers are differentiating work to meet their needs. An inspector may observe a withdrawal lesson or catch-up class. They can visit off-site provision. Inspectors may not spend long in one classroom. Instead, if they are looking at a theme – for example, attitudes and behaviour, or the progress shown in books of a particular ability group – they will flit between classes, spending perhaps only ten minutes in each class. One inspector will also usually talk to a group of pupils, not necessarily the School Council. To check on other pupils' perceptions, they will also chat to pupils at lunchtime, playtime/break, in corridors and lessons. Parents' questionnaires also feed into judgements on inclusion, especially where they have made comments. Parents are also able to (and do) telephone the lead inspector with concerns. The link governor for inclusion may not necessarily be interviewed, but the chair of governors generally will.

The final report is currently (2008) only 2,000 words long for secondary schools and 1,500 words for primaries. You will very likely find references to aspects of inclusion in each short section of the report, although there is no requirement for the written report to cover every judgement on the Inspection Judgement form. The final feedback is to the headteacher, together with any or all of the following: the senior leadership team, chair of governors, local authority advisor and School Improvement Partner. It is common for the team to give examples to back up their judgements at this point, and for the school managers to be able to ask questions for clarification. You will not get the subject-based feedback that you had under the pre-2005 inspection system. The headteacher will get a copy of the draft report for factual checking three working days after the end of the inspection.

Contributing to the Self-Evaluation Form

Writing the Self-Evaluation Form should involve the whole school, parents, governors and other stakeholders, and it should be part of a continuous process rather than a one-off. There is guidance at www.ofsted.gov.uk/assets/3950.doc, and the SEF form itself has prompts. Ofsted cannot insist on you using the online SEF, but if you don't, you will need to be able to give evidence of thorough self-evaluation. The quality and accuracy of self-evaluation usually reflects the quality of management. As part of the staff development of middle managers, many schools give each subject leader their own SEF to write. Because of the wide-ranging nature of your work as Inclusion Manager, you may find it useful to have contributions in each section of the whole-school SEF. The guidance on the website will help you. Ofsted recommend that you update the online SEF at least once a year. If it's a working document for your school, it will need to be updated perhaps more often.

Self-Evaluation Forms

Self-Evaluation Forms should evaluate rather than describe. After you have written a paragraph, try asking yourself, 'I have written that we do this. So what? How does this affect outcomes for our pupils? What evidence have we got for this?' Referring to the list of your evidence at the end of each section can be useful.

Self-Evaluation Forms are too long, often because they describe in detail rather than evaluate! The guidance recommends about 25 pages.

Many Self-Evaluation Forms repeat themselves in the sections on personal development and well-being and care, guidance and support (CGS) because the writer isn't clear about what the difference is. Personal development and well-being are the *outcomes*, while the care, guidance and support section describes the *inputs* – what the school provides. It is difficult to write the personal development section if you do not have any data. Do you ask different groups regularly their opinions on provision? What do mid-phase entrants think about induction, for example? The personal development section is where you can blow your trumpet about the social cohesion of your school. In the personal development and well-being section, the 'inadequate' descriptor now includes references to the isolation or integration of groups of learners.

From September 2009, academic guidance – the cycle of marking, assessment and target setting with pupils – is part of the teaching and learning section of the SEF. The care, guidance and support section is now more focused on pastoral care and guidance with options and future careers. This is where you are judged on how well the school prepares pupils for transitions, whether this is to the next key stage, to college, work or sixth form. Inspectors will probably want to look at a case study of how a vulnerable child has been supported in these ways.

Each of the sections is structured via a series of questions or prompts. Here is how one primary school responded; it is a little wordy, but it gives a good picture of an active, inclusive school.

Action taken to promote equality of opportunity, to ensure that all learners achieve good outcomes.

We work hard to ensure there is equality of opportunity and ensure all learners achieve good outcomes. We analyse the achievement and attainment of our children by gender, ethnicity, EAL, SEN, FSM and also length of time at the school, to identify any areas of underperformance. Support and interventions follow on from this. The Inclusion Manager has responsibility for the management of provision and support for pupils with SEN, EAL and G&T. She liaises with key-stage leaders and support staff to plan interventions for pupils, and monitors the impact of provision termly through pupil-tracking data. She organises staff meetings to write and review Individual Education Plans and Personal Support Plans, organises and delivers training, and liaises with governors. While class teachers write IEPs, the Inclusion Manager monitors teachers' SEN files to ensure IEPs are up to date and targets are appropriate. She also monitors the quality of support in classrooms and in intervention groups. Where pupil progress is limited, the Inclusion Manager will make a judgement about the best course of action. This may be a referral to an outside agency; meeting with the teacher and/or support assistant responsible, or a key professional from an outside agency to plan new strategies/interventions.

All children with SEN receive additional support either 1:1 or in small groups. Pupils with EAL are identified shortly after entry. There is support to pupils new to English through short-term 1:1 or small-group work with a specialist teacher. For more advanced bilingual learners, the Inclusion Manager monitors lesson planning and helps class teachers in identifying underachieving groups and introducing teaching strategies. She co-ordinates the induction of new EAL pupils, as well as organising International Evening and Refugee Week. The impact of her role is that across the school, no one particular ethnic group is underachieving. All staff plan for opportunities to develop language and provide explicit models to support the language needs of different learning activities. This has been a focus of lesson monitoring (evidence in lesson-monitoring file). The impact is that EAL pupils are achieving above the national average.

A register is kept of G&T pupils, but the emphasis is on enriching the curriculum for everyone. The Inclusion Manager liaises with subject leaders to ensure G&T pupils' needs are being met in class, supports class teachers in the analysis of data to ensure more able pupils are making at least good progress, and links with outside agencies to ensure they are involved in challenging extracurricular activities. The impact of the role is that at least 75 per cent of our pupils left Year 6 (2008) achieving level 5 in the core subjects.

Part C: Compliance with statutory requirements

At the back of the Self-Evaluation Form, there is this list of statutory requirements. The school must indicate whether they are fully in place, partly in place or not in place. If they are not fully in place, you must state what action is being taken to deal with that. The statutory requirements that I feel are particularly relevant to your job I have indicated *in italics*.

Table 8.1 Statutory requirements: the curriculum

	Fully in place	Partly in place	Not in place
1 *Every learner receives the full statutory curriculum that the school must provide.*			
2 The school provides teaching of religious education for all learners in accordance with the agreed syllabus or otherwise and has told parents/carers of the right to withdraw their children.			
3 Where the provider is a school, it provides a daily act of collective worship for all learners and has told parents/carers of the right to withdraw their children.			
4 (Schools with pupils of primary age) The governing body has decided whether or not to provide sex and relationships education and, if doing so, has agreed the content and organisation of the programme and has told parents/carers about it and the right to withdraw their children.			
5 (Schools with pupils of secondary age) The governing body has agreed the content and organisation of its programme of sex and relationships education and has told parents/carers about it and the right to withdraw their children.			
6 The school meets fully the learning and development requirements of the Early Years Foundation Stage (EYFS).			

Source: Ofsted Schools Self-Evaluation Form, HMSO 2009

Table 8.2 Statutory requirements: equality and diversity

	Fully in place	Partly in place	Not in place
7 *The governing body ensures that the provider does not discriminate unlawfully against learners, job applicants or staff on the grounds of sex, race, disability, gender, religion and belief or marital status.*			
8 *The governing body has agreed a written policy on race equality, arrangements to monitor its implementation and assess its impact on staff, learners and parents/carers and communicates the results of monitoring and assessments of impact to parents/ carers and the governing body.*			
9 *The school meets the requirements of the general duty and the specific duties in the Race Relations (Amendment) Act 2000 and the Commission for Racial Equality (CRE) code of practice.*			

Source: Ofsted Schools Self-Evaluation Form, HMSO 2009

From Ann Sydney (2010) *A Handbook for Inclusion Managers*, London: Routledge. © 2010 Ann Sydney

Table 8.3 Statutory requirements: learners with learning difficulties and disabilities

		Fully in place	Partly in place	Not in place
10	The school has regard to the Special Educational Needs Code of Practice when meeting learners' learning difficulties and/ or disabilities and makes its policy known to parents/carers.			
11	The school meets the requirements of the Special Educational Needs and Disability Act 2001 including Part 4 of the Disability Discrimination Act (DDA) code of practice for schools (2002) and any subsequent requirements. It has told parents/carers about its policy and arrangements and reports annually on the success of its special educational needs policy and the progress made in improving accessibility.			

Source: Ofsted Schools Self-Evaluation Form, HMSO 2009

Table 8.4 Statutory requirements: learners' care and well-being

		Fully in place	Partly in place	Not in place
12	The governing body has procedures for ensuring the provider meets all relevant health and safety regulations.			
13	The provider's procedures for child protection follow the requirements of the local Area Child Protection Committee, and the governing body ensures that these are followed.			
14	Where the governing body provide school lunches and/or other school food, they ensure that the nutritional standards meet the statutory requirements.			
15	The school meets the welfare requirements of the EYFS.			
16	The governing body fulfils the requirements to promote the well-being of pupils at the school.			

Source: Ofsted Schools Self-Evaluation Form, HMSO 2009

Table 8.5 Statutory requirements: informing parents/carers

		Fully in place	Partly in place	Not in place
17	The governing body ensures that all statutory assessments are conducted and results are forwarded to parents/carers and appropriate bodies.			
18	The governing body (of maintained schools only) ensures that each year a report on each learner's educational achievements is forwarded to their parents/carers.			

From Ann Sydney (2010) A Handbook for Inclusion Managers, London: Routledge. © 2010 Ann Sydney

Table 8.5 continued

	Fully in place	Partly in place	Not in place
19 *The school keeps parents and prospective parents/carers informed by publishing a school prospectus and by publishing a school profile in accordance with Regulations.*			

Source: Ofsted Schools Self-Evaluation Form, HMSO 2009

Table 8.6 Statutory requirements: leadership and management

	Fully in place	Partly in place	Not in place
20 The responsibilities of the governing body, its committees, the headteacher and staff in respect to finances are clearly defined and limits of delegated authority are delineated.			
21 The governing body has a performance management policy and ensures that all teachers, including the headteacher, are appraised in accordance with statutory requirements.			
22 The governing body has all relevant complaints and appeals procedures, as set out in the DfES guide to the law for school governors.			
23 *The governing body fulfils the requirements to promote community cohesion.*			
24 The provider meets the current government requirements regarding safeguarding children and safer recruitment.			
25 Where appropriate, the governing body has regard to the requirements of the Childcare Register.			

Source: Ofsted Schools Self-Evaluation Form, HMSO 2009

If the school does not comply, or only partly complies with statutory requirements, you are asked to explain what action is being taken to deal with that.

From Ann Sydney (2010) *A Handbook for Inclusion Managers*, London: Routledge. © 2010 Ann Sydney

Chapter 9

Writing the inclusion strategy

This is a short chapter because this is where the action happens. I have given an outline and in some cases examples to give a flavour, but the strategy will be different for every school. Now that you have a picture of what the legal framework is, where your school stands and where you want to be, you should be able to tackle a development plan for inclusion, or the inclusion strategy. This could be a freestanding document, or you might want it subsumed in the School Development Plan. The aim is to produce a document in plain English that will keep you on track. It does not have to be heavy enough to use as a doorstop. Keep it succinct and try to avoid the word 'ongoing'.

Essentially you need to plan what needs to be done, by whom, when, and where the resources for this will come from. The outcomes of performance measures or targets will indicate whether you are succeeding. You do not do it alone. Decide how you will involve parents and pupils. You will need the support of your bursar, governors and staff at different levels.

You could begin your work with them by producing a SWOT analysis together: What are the Strengths, Weaknesses, Opportunities and Threats that face your school on its journey towards inclusion? This will get everyone thinking strategically (and you may get new information). Threats might be high mobility, lack of funding, poor accommodation, anticipated but unknown changes. Opportunities might be strong, supportive leadership of the headteacher and governors, a strong, assertive discipline policy, effective provision for pupils with low-incidence additional needs at school cluster level . . . or many other things.

Introduction

Say why you are producing an inclusion strategy and how it fits with other school documentation.

Describe the context of your school and any particular issues that there are.

Set out the guiding principles of the strategy, such as taking a view of the whole child or provision being needs-led.

Say what outcomes you want from the strategy both in terms of the process (for example, everyone working together towards the same ends, or clear links between resources and targets) and in terms of measurable improvements (such as improved attendance, achievement of particular groups or better identification of pupils' additional needs). You need to clarify what evidence of impact you will be looking for.

You might set up a page under each of the following headings. This is broadly in line with the Ofsted inspection framework, but yours doesn't have to be; these are just ideas. Yours will relate to the issues in your school. I have inserted some examples just to give a flavour of what your planning might look like (see Tables 9.1 and 9.2).

Monitoring achievement and standards

This would cover pupil tracking; setting targets so that nothing is duplicated and no one is overburdened; target setting within the school's systems and with outside agencies; reviews and reports. It would also cover the strategic role of monitoring trends and the performance of groups.

Teaching and learning

What do you want to see in the classroom in terms of planning, differentiation and assessment for learning? How do you want extra support to be used? Look back at the section on 'Inclusive teaching and learning: What does it look like?'

This section could also cover clarifying the roles of different staff in identification, induction arrangements, communication across the school, referral procedures, tracking, CAF, how the school identifies and provides interventions, the range of assessments and use of data.

Curriculum

What would the ideal curriculum for the cohort look like this year? Next year? Does it cover every aspect of Every Child Matters including economic awareness? Does it offer personalised learning? Does the organisation of the school day and school year suit all groups of pupils? What other organisations can help to widen your curriculum, and how will you resource and review this?

Access and transitions

How far can you make your school accessible within the term of this strategy? Is any new building accessible?

What have you learned from last year's transitions, and how do you improve induction and preparation for leaving?

Leadership and management

Are all statutory requirements met? These are a priority for your strategy. How will you ensure this?

Is there a continuum of provision in your school?

Are service level agreements in place for working with other organisations?

Are referral processes clear? Is communication good enough?

Consultation

Who needs to see and comment on this before it is finalised? What is the timescale? You have expectations of a range of people inside and outside the school. Have they all contributed and been listened to?

Table 9.1 Identification and interventions

Issue for action	Evidence of impact	Lead staff	Resources	Timeline
Pupils with higher level EAL will be identified within one month of entry as part of induction procedure. Whole staff understanding of EAL will improve.	All staff will identify pupils with higher level EAL in lesson plans and match materials and teaching to their needs.	Inclusion manager.	One-session staff training with EAL specialist. Clerical staff add to database. Two dual-lesson observations by EAL specialist and IM or Head of English department. Book scrutiny Yrs 7, 9, 11 by English staff and EAL specialist. Staff meeting time for feedback. £ xxx	Autumn term 2008. Report back to whole staff January 2009. Part of induction procedure for new students from January 2008.

Table 9.2 Improving the curriculum for vulnerable pupils

Issue for action	Evidence of impact	Lead staff	Resources	Timeline
Use assessment data to improve the curriculum planning and provision for vulnerable groups.	Test results for identified pupils will improve. Pupils will voice greater satisfaction with the curriculum.	Inclusion manager.	One-session staff training on use of external and internal data. Meetings with Deputy Head (curriculum). Visit to local leading school. Involve pupils in monitoring the curriculum (TASC wheel system). Inclusion Manager to check long-term and mid-term planning. Staff meeting to evaluate changes. £ xxx	Spring term 2010. New curriculum in place September 2010. Evaluation and modifications September 2011.

Implementation

Say how this will happen. Which people will oversee different sections, and are any resources earmarked? Does this strategy's timelines fit in with the school development plan?

Review

Who will check that things are moving towards the desired outcomes fast enough? How often will they check? How will stakeholders be involved?

Chapter 10

Writing the inclusion policy

Guidelines

Now you know what your school is like, where you want to be and how you are going to get there. In the inclusion policy, you will show all stakeholders and the outside world your level of commitment to inclusion.

Your inclusion policy need not be more than a few pages. You already have a special educational needs policy and an access plan.

Your policy might usefully begin with a definition of 'inclusion' and a statement of the school's intent.

Some description of the context the school is working within would be helpful to anyone not familiar with it.

Parents and carers will want some reassurance about the admissions procedure and access.

Describe the range of provision for your pupils, including transitions and any interesting features of the curriculum. One way of presenting this section would be to frame it around the five areas of Every Child Matters:

- Be healthy.
- Stay safe.
- Enjoy and achieve.
- Make a positive contribution to the community.
- Achieve economic well-being.

Under each heading, say what the school has done. For example, under 'Making a positive contribution', one sentence might be: 'All pupils learn about disability issues in PSHE lessons in Year 7.'

Say how you check on the quality of provision.

Parents, carers and school users will also want to know what to do if they are unhappy with what the school is doing and the name of a contact person.

Date the policy and say when it will be reviewed.

To avoid making the policy too long, signpost links in the inclusion policy to other school documents. Put it on your website.

Examples from primary and secondary schools

The following are two examples of an inclusion policy: one from Brindishe primary school in Lewisham, and the other from South Camden Community School, a large inner-London comprehensive. They both show a thoughtful approach and a very real commitment to inclusion. Please treat these as examples and not prescriptions; your school is unique.

Example I

Reproduced with the kind permission of Vicki Paterson, executive headteacher of Brindishe and Hither Green primary schools, London borough of Lewisham.

Brindishe primary school inclusion policy

We welcome and celebrate difference, diversity and individuality at Brindishe. For us, inclusion means making sure that everyone who is part of our community can easily understand, access, feel part of and benefit from all that the school can offer. More than this, it means doing all we can to recognise and remove or overcome barriers to learning, achievement and well-being, and to work towards ensuring that children of all abilities have their learning needs met.

Brindishe children, families and staff are from a rich variety of social backgrounds, family structures, ethnic groups and religions. We are opposed to any form of discrimination or exclusion and will actively work to ensure that all adults and children are given every opportunity to achieve, to recognise their own worth and to play an important part in our community.

This policy helps to ensure that this school promotes and appreciates the individuality of all our children, irrespective of ethnicity, attainment, age, disability, gender or family background. The different aspects of this policy are interrelated and should be considered and implemented together.

Our key aims are:

* to enable children to live, play and learn harmoniously;
* to help children learn that difference and diversity are valued and welcome;
* to make sure that success in school is not dependent upon being able bodied, belonging to any particular culture, gender, social class, sexual orientation, family circumstance or majority group;
* to make sure every adult in school is able to fulfil their role without hindrance and with every support and assistance.

OUR GUIDING PRINCIPLES AT BRINDISHE

To achieve these aims, we all support and apply the following guiding principles to help us make decisions, to evaluate the impact of our work and to inform the way that we act individually and collectively as members of the Brindishe School community:

* Children are valued as individuals and encouraged and enabled to be confident, successful and open-minded learners.
* Families, children, staff and governors work together to set and meet high standards of attendance, learning and behaviour.

- We oppose all prejudice, discrimination and exclusive practices, and work to ensure that everyone is regarded as important in our community.
- Staff and governors ensure that they are knowledgeable, fair, adaptable, well organised and that they continue to develop expertise.
- We always provide a high-quality learning environment and an inclusive and wide-ranging curriculum.
- We will always make clear, open and effective decisions that best support children's learning.

These aims and principles also relate to the government's Every Child Matters agenda, with its aim for every child, whatever their background or their circumstances, to have the support they need in order to:

- Be healthy.
- Stay safe.
- Enjoy and achieve.
- Make a positive contribution.
- Achieve economic well-being.

BEING AWARE AND BEING CLEAR

We are aware of institutional racism, discrimination, stereotyping and exclusive language and practices. We know that we all make assumptions that are not helpful and mistakes that are insensitive. To counter this, we keep ourselves well trained and informed and make ourselves ever more aware so that we can address our shortcomings positively and openly. We must all directly challenge what we understand to be bias, discrimination, exclusion, prejudice and harassment. We address equality issues through a broad and balanced creative curriculum. In particular we use PSHME (personal, social, health and moral education) and citizenship teaching to promote personal development and positive practices. This policy also links closely to our behaviour and positive relationships policy.

In order that we are all clear, we work to the following definitions:

- Discrimination is the practice of treating a person or group of people less favourably than others because of an assumption that their needs, lifestyle, culture or practices are less important or less acceptable than others.
- Prejudice is pre-judging people or groups of people on the basis of false assumptions or inadequate evidence. The judgement is usually negative and involves holding opinions or having attitudes which are not founded in fact.
- Institutional discrimination is the *collective* failure of an organisation (such as a school) to provide an appropriate and professional service to people because of their colour, religion, sexuality, lifestyle, gender, ethnic origin or physical appearance. It can be seen in practices, attitudes and behaviour (things you do and things you say) that discriminate through prejudice, ignorance, thoughtlessness and stereotyping and that disadvantage certain individuals or groups of individuals.
- It is possible for an institution and individual to discriminate by *not* doing something as well as by doing something. It is discriminating to ignore, omit, disregard, make invisible or 'gloss over' an important aspect or feature of a person's life or community.

- Harassment is a form of bullying where the intention is to cause insult or injury or harm for specific reasons connected to the recipient's *identity or culture*. It is more than bullying – it is bullying a person because that person is, for example, female, gay, black, disabled.

EXCLUSIVE LANGUAGE OR PRACTICES

This is a way of behaving or speaking which makes *some* people feel included and *some* people feel left out. It may be careless or intentional but it nearly always involves an assumption that the audience or recipient has the same perspective as you or belongs to the same group as you or feels or responds in the same way that you do. It always makes the recipient feel 'other' or 'odd' or in some way 'deficient'. Examples are:

- asking children 'Where did you go for your summer holiday?' without acknowledging that the group includes children for whom a holiday was not possible;
- saying to a class of children 'I'm sure everyone's mum and dad will want to come along';
- only serving wine, beer, tea and coffee at a school family function.

Here is an example of an 'exclusive practice' on an application form:

- asking father's name or father's occupation;
- asking mother's name or mother's occupation.

INCLUSIVE LANGUAGE OR PRACTICES

This is a way of behaving or speaking which makes *all* people feel included and *no one* feel left out. It never assumes that the audience or recipient has the same perspective as you or belongs to the same group as you or feels or responds in the same way that you do. It needs careful thought but can readily and easily be learnt. It needs empathy and a conscious appreciation of the uniqueness of each individual. Examples are:

- asking children 'Tell me one thing that you enjoyed during the summer holiday';
- saying to a class of children, 'Ask your adults at home if they'd like to come along';
- making sure that you always offer non-alcoholic and non-stimulant drinks at a school family function too.

Here is an example of an 'inclusive practice' on an application form:

- parent carer 1 and parent carer 2 (if appropriate).

MAKING SURE PLACES AT BRINDISHE ARE ALLOCATED FAIRLY AND TRANSPARENTLY

We follow the published Admissions Policy for Lewisham Children and Young People's Services. A copy of our published policy is freely available from the school office or from:

Primary Admissions Team
Lewisham Directorate for Children and Young People
3rd floor Laurence House
1 Catford Road
London SE6 4RU.

If you would like help in understanding the policy or in completing an application form, please ask in the school office. We can also arrange a translation service for you.

ACCESS AND ENTITLEMENT TO LEARNING

All children aged 3–5 in Brindishe School will be supported in moving towards the Early Learning Goals. These are based on six areas of learning (knowledge and understanding of the world; communication, language and literacy; mathematical development; physical development; creative development; personal, social and emotional development), and our curriculum will be designed to enable all children to learn and develop in these areas.

From Year 1 (the year in which children become aged 6), all children are entitled to access the National Curriculum: English, Mathematics, Science, History, Geography, Design and technology, Information and communication technology (ICT), Art, Music, PE and also RE. In Brindishe we also offer all children access to an extended curriculum which includes areas such as environmental education, citizenship, a modern foreign language and sex education.

All children in Year 2 (the year in which children become aged 7) and Year 6 (the year in which children become aged 11) are entitled to be assessed according to national arrangements for assessment.

PERSONALISED LEARNING

We are committed to personalised learning for all children.

Personalisation is the key to tackling the persistent achievement gaps between different social and ethnic groups. It means a tailored education for every child and high-quality teaching that is responsive to the different ways in which children achieve their best. It means taking a responsive approach to each child's learning, shaping teaching around the different ways in which children learn in order that all are able to progress, achieve and participate. It means strengthening the link between learning and teaching by engaging children, and their parents, as partners in learning.

We provide a curriculum that is broad, rich, inclusive and relevant. The main focus at Brindishe is to create an achievement culture, providing the right opportunities, with support and encouragement, to each child in order to develop a desire to learn and to achieve as much as possible. We present children with learning that challenges, stretches and excites them on a daily basis, in an environment that celebrates excellence. We celebrate both effort and achievement across the curriculum.

We aim to make learning vivid and real, developing understanding through enquiry, creativity, e-learning and problem solving, within and beyond the classroom. We make learning an enjoyable and challenging experience, using a variety of teaching styles and matching tasks to learners' maturity and preferred learning styles.

We enrich the learning experience by making links across the curriculum. We make appropriate provision that stretches children in areas of strength and develops them in areas of relative weakness.

Children:

- are treated as partners in their learning, with joint responsibility for participating in the design of their learning;
- have their individual needs addressed, both in school and extending beyond the classroom and into the family and community;
- are able to identify their weaknesses and how to improve, if they start to fall behind in their learning, and will be given additional support to help them get back on track quickly;
- receive co-ordinated support to enable them to succeed to the full, whatever their talent or background;
- develop skills for collaboration through learning in a mutually supportive environment.

Families:

- receive regular updates that give clear understanding of what their child can currently do, how they can progress and what help can be given at home;
- are involved in engaging with their child's learning and in planning their future education;
- are confident that their child is receiving a high-quality education that is designed to meet their learning needs and that will equip them with the skills they need to thrive throughout their lives;
- have the opportunity to play a more active role in school life and know that their contribution is valued.

Teachers and support staff:

- have high expectations of every learner, and use a range of teaching strategies to give them the confidence and skills to succeed;
- have access to and are able to interpret data on each pupil to inform teaching and learning;
- are in a strong position to share and exchange information about best practice among their colleagues in different schools and through external networks, resulting in opportunities to develop a wide repertoire of teaching strategies;
- participate in high-quality professional development, working with other teachers to develop their skills in understanding the learning needs of their children and how best to address those needs and engage them;
- are able to depend on each other and on other adults from outside the school to provide a holistic, tailored educational provision for all their children;
- put personalising learning at the heart of their vision for transforming teaching and learning;
- accept and assume that every child comes into the classroom with a different knowledge base and skill set, as well as varying aptitudes and aspirations.

ENRICHMENT

We also offer a variety of activities that take place outside children's normal learning times and are offered in addition to the primary school curriculum. Details about after-school clubs, tuition and activities may be obtained from the school office or via the weekly newsletter. After- and out-of-school clubs and tuition are activities that take place after school, at lunchtime and very occasionally at weekends.

For some clubs there is a cost for tuition. We aim to keep the cost generally very low. Children whose parents are unable to pay for clubs are not excluded; the fee is waived or subsidised for children of low-income families. This is supported through fund-raising or through our voluntary school fund.

Year groups or classes are offered the opportunity to join a club or take up tuition, and where there is over-subscription, staff will select names to ensure that there is a balanced and fair distribution. This might be, for example, of boys and girls, of ability levels or of age groups. We will use selection to avoid the situation whereby some children have several opportunities while others have none. We try to avoid offering differing types of activity (e.g., football and choir) on the same day so that we can avoid conflict of interests.

CREATIVE ENTITLEMENT

We ensure entitlement to creative and cultural learning opportunities for all children. This could be an opportunity to work with a well-known author or a skilled artist or musician, opportunities to take part in a wide range of extra-curricular activities or through a visit to a place beyond the local environment. We track access to clubs, visits, visitors, video-conferencing, performances, school journey programmes, etc., in order to ensure a balance for all different groups of children. No child is prevented from taking part in these opportunities because of an inability to pay.

BARRIERS TO LEARNING

Barriers to learning may be related to:

- emotional and social development and behaviour;
- communication and interaction skills;
- physical, motor and sensory skills;
- cognition and learning.

These aspects are often inter-related.

ATTENDANCE

All children have the right to their education and to arrive and leave school at the appropriate time each day. Research shows that children who attend school regularly do better at school and make better progress. We monitor attendance and punctuality for all children and keep careful records, and we will always take action if a child does not attend regularly or there are concerns about reasons for non-attendance.

MEDICAL NEEDS

We are committed to supporting children with specific health conditions in an appropriate and consistent manner. Parents/carers are encouraged to provide the school with full information about their child's medical needs. Any medical information is treated confidentially. We work together to ensure equality of access for all, and we recognise that medical conditions, if not properly managed, can limit a child's access to education.

INCREASING ACCESS TO LEARNING

We recognise that some children need increased access to learning. Children are given access to additional learning support if they have a significantly greater difficulty in learning than the majority of children of the same age. They also access increased support if they have a disability that gets in the way of them being able to access and benefit from the educational opportunities generally enjoyed by children of the same age.

At Brindishe we use the term 'learning support' in place of 'special needs'. This describes the additional or different help or resources that a child may need to support their learning. It involves identifying and, if possible, removing barriers to learning and increasing a child's ability to participate and be successful in learning. We think that many barriers to learning can be removed or minimised by careful thought about where the learner is, what the learner has been asked to do and what they are expected to achieve. We constantly develop and use a range of strategies and resources to remove barriers to learning and to help each learner to make progress.

Provision for children who require learning support is a responsibility for the school as a whole. Targets are set for these children and then reviewed regularly and shared with their parents. Their needs are met as part of the continuous cycle of planning, teaching and assessment that takes place for all children. The class teacher remains responsible for working with, and planning for, each and every child. Everyone at Brindishe can help someone else to learn – and that is what we all expect of each other. We also see families as partners, actively involved in a child's learning.

RESOURCING FOR LEARNING SUPPORT

Schools are funded according to the number of children on-roll and are given an amount of money to support children who have additional educational needs. Some funding for children is delegated to the local collaborative of schools. This is a network of seven local primary schools who work together to develop projects/services, support children and extend experiences. It might be used to provide support or a resource across the collaborative – for example, additional speech and language therapy provision.

Each April the full governing body of the school discusses the budget and agrees the amount and type of staffing that can be afforded in the current financial year. This includes the number of teachers and the number of hours of additional classroom support.

Once staffing levels have been decided, the headteacher and inclusion team leader plan the allocation of support for individuals and groups of children in consultation with teaching staff, using information from the learning support register and data on performance and achievement of each year group.

We also use our budget to fund:

- books and materials;
- training and training materials;
- administration (record keeping, writing individual action plans, communication, etc);
- time for liaison between teacher and support staff, the inclusion team leader, headteacher and parents and support services such as the school doctor, educational psychologist and speech therapists;
- specialist advice and support (e.g., counselling, therapy, mentoring).

Some children will have a statement of special need. This means they will have additional and targeted resources (money) to provide additional 1:1 support for the child and to buy specialist advice or resources. We review and monitor how this is used to make sure we are deploying the resources to good effect. Parents, children and staff contribute to the review process.

GIFTED AND TALENTED LEARNERS

We define gifted and talented children as children 'who achieve, or have the ability to achieve, at a level significantly in advance of the average for their year group'. This is nationally expected to be around 10 per cent of each year group. The term 'gifted' is used to refer to children capable of excelling in academic subjects; 'talented' is used for those who may excel in areas of the curriculum requiring visual/spatial skills or practical abilities, such as in games and PE, drama, music or art and design.

We identify and assess gifted and talented children at Brindishe by using professional judgement and evidence from a variety of sources including:

- baseline information from the Foundation Stage profile;
- classroom observation;
- assessment for learning;
- standardised tests and national curriculum results;
- midterm reviews;
- evidence from children's learning;
- evidence from extra-curricular and out-of-school activities;
- parental observations;
- subject specific checklists;
- peer group nominations.

We regularly review and refresh our identification processes in the light of pupil performance and value-added data, and we monitor to ensure that it reflects our school population and that both genders and different ethnic and social groups are represented.

We provide a range of challenging teaching and learning strategies, including:

- varied and flexible grouping within a year group;
- vertical grouping across year groups when appropriate;
- withdrawal of very able children for higher-level work within small groups;

- upward differentiation/extension in schemes of work;
- teaching thinking skills in a subject context, e.g., problem solving and decision-making;
- asking higher-order questions that encourage investigation and enquiry;
- setting clear and challenging targets;
- enabling children to evaluate their own and others' work;
- a wide range of extra-curricular activities and clubs;
- opportunities for artistic, musical, dramatic and sporting development.

We frequently review our resources to ensure that we have up-to-date and relevant materials to be used with more able children. We continue to extend materials that can be used to support the development of philosophy, enquiry and thinking skills.

The main focus at Brindishe is to create an achievement culture, providing the right opportunities, with support and encouragement, to each child in order to develop a desire to learn and to achieve as much as possible. We present children with learning that challenges, stretches and excites them on a daily basis, in an environment that celebrates excellence. We celebrate both effort and achievement across the curriculum.

TREATING BOYS AND GIRLS AND MEN AND WOMEN EQUALLY (GENDER EQUALITY)

We are proactive and we promote gender equality. We have a gender equality policy, and within this we have a three-year action plan to outline our priorities and targets and the ways in which we will fulfil our gender equality commitments.

We are committed to ensuring equality of education and opportunity for all, irrespective of gender. We work to eliminate discrimination in employment practice and actively promote gender equality within our workforce. We encourage parents/carers of both genders to participate in their child's education. The achievement of all children is monitored on the basis of gender. We look for developing trends and patterns, and we use this data to raise standards and ensure inclusive teaching. We aim to provide our learners with a firm foundation that will enable them to fulfil their potential, regardless of gender. We actively challenge gender stereotypes, and we encourage both boys and girls to take a full and active part in all areas of school life, including extra-curricular clubs and activities.

DISABILITY EQUALITY

We do not treat disabled children or adults less favourably than their non-disabled peers, and we make reasonable adjustments to ensure that school users who are disabled are not put at a substantial disadvantage in comparison to those who are not disabled. We will provide auxiliary aids and written material in alternative formats to ensure access to information, resources and support.

We have a disability equality policy, and within this we have an action plan to outline our targets for meeting requirements. We plan strategically to increase access to school premises to all users and access to the curriculum for children with disabilities. This is known as our accessibility plan. It is intended to ensure that we work towards the position wherein all children and adults with disabilities are enabled to take as full and active a part in this school as possible. We plan to extend our ability to meet the needs of children and adults with disabilities.

Current plans include the following improvements that we want to make to the school building and grounds:

* providing disabled access to the playground;
* redesigning all of the available play spaces for children so that we can meet children's differing needs and abilities;
* installing appropriate handles and mechanisms to taps and door handles;
* making our website more accessible.

RACE EQUALITY, ETHNICITY AND CULTURAL DIVERSITY

We define racism as a belief that members of some races are superior or inferior to others. We provide a culture and ethos in which everyone feels safe and valued. We try to engender a sense of belonging among every member of the school community. We celebrate cultural, religious and ethnic diversity. Diversity is seen as an opportunity not a reason for under-achievement. We focus on data collected and analysed by ethnicity, and we use this data to improve the quality of our provision and to inform the effective deployment of resources.

We value the individuality of all our children and believe that every pupil should be helped to develop a sense of personal and cultural identity that is confident and open to change, and that is receptive and respectful towards differing identities. We are committed to giving all our children every opportunity to achieve the highest standards and to develop the knowledge, understanding and skills they need in order to equip them for their future life. Within this ethos of achievement, we do not tolerate bullying or harassment of any kind. We aim to reflect the multi-ethnic nature of our society and ensure that the education we offer fosters positive attitudes to all people.

In order to do this we:

* include and draw upon images, artefacts and texts from a wide variety of cultures and traditions;
* make every effort to find out about the variety of cultures to which children and adults belong and to share this with our school community.

We will work to ensure that all school users feel part of the school community and see their cultures represented in our curriculum. We will seek to include a multi-cultural, multi-faith perspective in planning all areas of the curriculum. We will encourage the representation of different ethnic groups on the school staff, governing body and PHAB (partnership of home and Brindishe).

All staff at Brindishe are committed to responding to and dealing with any racist incidents in accordance with our clear guidelines and expectations as published in our protocol for responding to racist incidents.

ENGLISH AS AN ADDITIONAL LANGUAGE (EAL)

We have a significant number of school users who use English as an additional language. We recognise that cultural and linguistic diversity is a rich resource for the whole school.

We also recognise that children's achievement is linked to a welcoming environment in which they feel valued and confident. Building on children's knowledge of other cultures and languages, we will support EAL learners in becoming confident speakers and writers of English in all areas of the curriculum. Learning an additional language may present a challenge to curriculum access but must not be confused with learning difficulties. However, we also strive to ensure that we do not overlook any learning difficulties that EAL learners might have.

We will access translation and interpreting services in order to ensure that we communicate effectively with parents/carers whose first language is not English. We also work to ensure that texts and resources reflect the variety of languages in order to support and encourage bilingual children and also to raise general awareness of this variety.

SOCIO-ECONOMIC STATUS

A family's socio-economic status is based on family income, parental education, parental occupation and social status in the community. Recent research shows that socio-economic status is the biggest factor affecting attainment for children of both genders and from all ethnic backgrounds. At Brindishe we use our comprehensive tracking system to monitor the progress of children from different socio-economic backgrounds. Through this we look for developing trends and patterns, and we use this data to continue to raise standards and to ensure inclusive teaching. Above all, we maintain and encourage high expectations for all our learners, regardless of their backgrounds. We recognise that children learn more successfully when their families are interested in what they are doing at school.

In order to gain the views of all members of our community, we consult families in as many ways as possible. This includes making time to talk issues through in order to ensure that everyone is fully informed.

Before a child starts school in Nursery or Reception, we visit families at home to discuss and share information. This helps us to understand each child's home circumstances and to build on their experiences once they join us. We show appreciation of what families have already done and continue to do at home.

We ensure that children from different socio- economic groups have access to the full range of educational opportunities at Brindishe. We believe that financial difficulty should not be a barrier to children's participation and enjoyment of enriching experiences such as school trips, school journey and our wide range of extra-curricular clubs and activities, if necessary offering reduced-cost or free opportunities. We lend suitable clothing such as a PE kit or a warm coat if, for any reason, a child does not have one.

We work hard to reach out to and involve families so that they feel comfortable and valued within school. We are sensitive to individual needs and try to be flexible. We get to know names so that we can greet and welcome people personally. When parent meetings are held, they are often rescheduled in order to accommodate differing parental needs. We find different ways to communicate with those who are less confident about their literacy skills. We do not make assumptions about family situations, saying, for example, 'Go home and look it up on the internet', or 'Bring your bike to school tomorrow for our sponsored cycle'.

We keep our focus on learning at all times, and we enable and encourage children and their families to have high expectations and aspirations.

Where possible and appropriate, we put families in contact with other agencies who may be able to offer them some additional support, such as the school nurse, child and adolescent mental health services (CAMHS) or social care and health.

We recognise the value of a truly inclusive school where children learn, mix and become friends with others of differing abilities and from a range of different family backgrounds and circumstances.

Our Friends of Brindishe has been re-launched as PHAB (partnership of home and Brindishe). This has been in order to widen its scope and to ensure that as many people as possible, from a wide variety of backgrounds, can be involved in a range of different ways.

We have also extended the make up of our school council beyond peer nomination so that staff may nominate children. In this way we can ensure a balance of different abilities and socio-economic, cultural and faith groups, in order that the children's voice is more representative of the school population as a whole.

RESPONDING POSITIVELY TO DIFFERENT OR NON-TRADITIONAL FAMILY STRUCTURES

There are many different family structures in our community. We do not assume that a child has both mother and father at home. Children may have step- or foster families, live with lone parents or same-gender parents or be brought up by grandparents. They may spend part of the week with one parent and part of the week with another. We make sure that we are aware of and communicate with all those who parent or who have responsibility for the child. This includes, for example, sending a copy of the report to more than one parent, sending newsletters to two home addresses for one child, knowing and using the preferred name and title of the carer.

DISCRIMINATION AGAINST GAY AND LESBIAN PEOPLE

There are many gay and lesbian people in our community, and we recognise the existence of and damage caused by homophobia in society and among our community. We will not tolerate it in our school. Homophobia among adults is classified as a hate crime, and incidents may be reported to the police. Homophobia in and among children is much more likely to be about their lack of understanding. It is usually a learned response and not a considered view or opinion based on experience. In short, it is prejudice.

We do not allow or support discrimination or prejudice or accept language or behaviour that is harmful or negative or less than respectful to any individual person or group of people. We always respond in a consistent, clear and positive way in dealing with any and all kinds of homophobia or homophobic name calling in school. We will enable children and young adults to understand that there are a range of options and choices in people's sexuality, lifestyle and partner preference, and that our differences are valid and valued and recognised.

We make sure that children understand that the words 'gay' and 'lesbian' describe people. We help children understand that being gay or lesbian is about more than sexual preference (just as ethnicity is about more than skin tone). We help children to understand that the words gay and lesbian are not terms of abuse or ridicule and they are not 'rude' or swearing.

RECRUITMENT AND EMPLOYMENT

We advertise all job vacancies and we follow Lewisham Council's Equal Opportunities Policy in relation to job applications and the recruitment process.

We work to eliminate discrimination in employment practice and actively promote equality within our workforce.

BRINDISHE GOVERNING BODY

Our governors usually hold office for four years. The governing body is made up as follows:

- four parent governors who are elected by the parent community;
- three staff governors, one of whom will be the headteacher;
- three community governors who are invited to join in order to widen the expertise or perspective of the governing body;
- three local authority governors who are appointed by Lewisham's mayor and cabinet.

Governors meetings are open to all members of the school community, who may come as observers. Observers are asked to inform the governing body of their intention to attend a meeting.

The governing body ensures that:

- the school complies with race relations, disability, gender and SEN-related legislation, including the general and specific duties;
- this policy and all its related procedures and strategies are implemented;
- monitoring is undertaken in relation to ethnicity, language, attainment, age, disability, gender and family background, and that action is taken based on any outcomes;
- this policy is reviewed regularly and kept up to date.

Regular review of this policy will be undertaken. We will monitor the effects of this policy on different groups and take action based on any outcomes.

MAKING SURE OUR POLICY WORKS

Governors and staff actively seek support from the whole school community in achieving the aims set out in this policy. Our commitment will be demonstrated through:

- monitoring the impact of all our policies on different groups including ethnicity, gender, class, disability, etc.;
- monitoring and addressing issues relating to pupil progress, attainment and assessment;
- monitoring and addressing issues relating to behaviour and exclusion;
- ensuring high expectations for all;

- drawing on the diverse experiences and skills of all staff, children and the wider community;
- removing barriers in order to maximise participation and achievement for all;
- providing training for staff so that they are confident in promoting equality and in challenging any form of discrimination;
- seeking views from all stakeholders and from children in relation to the range of issues around equality and inclusion through questionnaires, in school planning reviews, governors' open house, at parents' evenings and through focus group discussions.

Approved: September 2008   For review: September 2010

Example 2

Reproduced with the kind permission of Rosemary Leeke, headteacher, South Camden Community School, London borough of Camden.

Inclusion policy and framework

> An educationally inclusive school is one in which the teaching and learning achievements and attitudes and well-being of every young person matter. Effective schools are educationally inclusive schools. This shows, not only in their performance but also in their ethos and their willingness to offer new opportunities to pupils who may have experienced previous difficulties. This does not mean treating all pupils the same way. Rather, it involves taking account of pupils' varied life experiences and needs.
>
> (Ofsted 2001)

SCCS inclusion statement

In South Camden Community School we believe we are an effective school because we are an inclusive school. We have no selection criteria for admission to our school apart from that determined by the LEA local admissions policy.

The proportion of our students entitled to free school meals is recognised as being well above the national average. A very high percentage of our students, 81 per cent, do not have English as their first language. The percentage of students with special educational needs is above the national average and of those with statements of special educational need is well above the national average.

Within this context our support for learning and inclusion is very significant. The teaching and learning, achievements, attitudes and well-being of every young person matter in our school.

It is within this context that we have developed a policy framework and mapped the provision through which we aim to support the inclusion and achievement of a number of students with a vast range of need.

This framework represents our inclusion policy in action. It is through this framework, that we aim to make a difference to the lives of students who attend our school.

Provision

We have developed a range of provision within South Camden Community School that helps support the learning and inclusion of a number of students with a vast range of need. The provision includes:

- SEN Provision to support students with additional and/or different learning needs.
- A Special Educational Needs Co-ordinator (SENCO) who manages a combined team of five support teachers (including the teacher in charge of the Resource Base) and 16 teaching assistants.
- A Resource Base for students with physical disabilities and associated learning needs. This has provision for nine students and is supported by a teacher with a designated responsibility to support the inclusion of students with physical disabilities and associated learning needs, in the curriculum. The Resource Base also has six identified teaching assistants who support the medical, physical and learning needs of students throughout the school day.

(See Provision Map and access plan)
This combined team offers a range of support:

- in-class support within curriculum areas for students with Statements and students on the Code of Practice for Special Needs;
- withdrawal from class for individual and small group literacy support;
- support for the implementation of agreed physiotherapy and or occupational therapy programmes;
- withdrawal for identified individual learning programmes to support inclusion.

(See SEN Policy, Provision Map and Teaching and Learning Policy)
Behaviour Provision – through the Learning Support Unit and Internal Exclusion Room to support behaviour improvement across the school and the inclusion of students with behaviour that challenges.

This is a provision led by a teacher in charge of the LSU, assisted by an additional behaviour support teacher; one behaviour support teaching assistant and two Behaviour Improvement (BIP) mentors.

This combined Behaviour Improvement Team support students who:

- have poor anger management skills;
- have difficulty with sanctions;
- are aggressive, insolent or belligerent;
- lack respect for authority;
- have poor social and communication skills;
- lack self esteem and confidence.

(See Behaviour Policy and LSU and IER provisions)
Our Behaviour Support staff support the management of student behaviour across the school alongside all staff who implement our Behaviour Policy and whole school agreed behaviour code, Behaviour for Learning (see also Provision Map).

EMAG Provision – to support the needs of minority ethnic students including recent arrivals, refugees and asylum seekers. (See Language Policy, Provision Map, Race Equality Policy and access plan.)

This provision is led by the Head of Ethnic Minority Achievement. It includes a Refugee Co-ordinator and four additional language support teachers. The team also includes two Home School Link workers for the Bengali and Somali communities as well as a part time Induction Mentor to support students who arrive in school after the beginning of an academic year. The EMAG team work closely with advisory teachers from the Camden Language Support Service (CLASS) in identifying underachieving groups of students and targeting additional support and provision.

We recognise that for a significant minority of students in school a lack of fluency in English is a barrier to their learning. As part of our commitment to their inclusion we provide, in the first instance, an induction programme to support students for whom English is a new language. Following assessment, students are reintegrated into mainstream lessons on a full-time basis and are further supported to develop their English language skills through a focus on acquiring language across the curriculum.

Other strands of support for learning and inclusion are:

- Gifted and Talented Provision, which offers extension opportunities for our gifted and talented students. It is managed by a co-ordinator and line-managed by a member of the Leadership team. This provision supports staff to ensure that their teaching provides gifted and talented students with sufficient challenge and stimulus to achieve to their potential. (See Gifted and Talented Policy.)
- Sixth Form Provision. All students from the SCCS Year 11 cohort who have the appropriate qualifications are admitted to the Sixth Form. The admission requirements for students wishing to take AS or AVCE courses have been maintained at 5/4 GCSE's at A*–C grade respectively. The Sixth Form offer currently includes an Entry Level EAL course, a new Level 1 (or Foundation) offer with the main objectives including supporting basic skills and offering individual student progression and Level 2 Intermediate GNVQ courses which offer progression into related courses at Level 3.
- We make available a substantial guidance programme together with an Aim Higher programme through which we aim to support students in making appropriate and aspirational progression choices. Evidence of the success of this programme is a large increase in the numbers of students gaining University places and the higher grades required for many of those places. There is a focus currently on developing further our vocational guidance for students not wishing to enter Higher Education or for whom Higher Education is not appropriate. There is also additional focus on the support for students with statements of special educational need who are now attending the Sixth Form.

Additional strands of support for learning and inclusion are:

- A learning mentor team with a Lead Mentor and two additional mentors to support students who are underachieving in school and at risk of disaffection. We also work closely with UCL academic mentors who work with underachieving students as well as business mentors.

- Full-time Educational Welfare Officer (EWO) and full-time Attendance Officer support for improving attendance and punctuality.
- Connexions Provision and Personal Advisors. This provision is lead by the Head of Business Education and Work-Related Learning and involves two Connexions Advisors with one designated on a part-time basis to support the specific needs of students who are refugees and asylum seekers. This provision also benefits from the additional support of a Careers advisor on a weekly basis.
- Counsellors in School. We benefit from a weekly allocation of time from two Brief Therapists who offer Solution-Focussed Therapy to support the needs of students. Students can make individual requests for counselling, or they can be referred by tutors and/or Year Co-ordinators through our Pastoral Review Forum, to receive counselling.
- Child and Adolescent Mental Health Service (CAMHS). We have the additional support of a mental health professional based in school two days per week. Referrals for support are discussed and made at our multi-agency weekly Pastoral Review Forum. Referrals can arise from parental and/or student request, concerns being raised about a student by tutors and/or Year Co-ordinators, learning mentors or support staff working closely with a student. The CAMHS professional on behalf of the school liaises with appropriate agencies linked to supporting students with mental health support needs and can advise on the need for referrals of students and families to support from agencies outside of the school.

Further support for learning and inclusion from outside agencies includes:

- support from the Behaviour Educational Support Team available through BIP;
- an Educational Psychologist (40 Sessions);
- Behaviour Support Teacher (BSS) – one morning weekly;
- Behaviour Support Social Worker (BSS) – as required;
- Crime and Truancy Officer – as required;
- the Traveller Education Support Team;
- an Additional Support Teacher – weekly support for individual students.

As part of the Safer Schools Partnership, we have a Safer Schools Partnership Officer in school throughout the week. This provision supports us in our efforts to address and reduce incidents of crime and anti-social behaviour with the school and local community. (See Safer Schools Protocol and Inclusive Education Faculty Chart.)

Identification and management

Through our year team meetings, Year Co-ordinators identify students presenting with issues that create a barrier to their learning and inclusion. They bring these issues to the Pastoral Review Forum for discussion and consideration of targeted support.

The efficient use and deployment of a vast range of resources and support for inclusion is made possible through the work of our Pastoral Support Team involving an Assistant Headteacher (Inclusion), the Year Co-ordinators for Years 7–11 as well as all relevant professionals, the SENCO, Refugee Co-ordinator, Education Welfare Officer, Lead Mentor, CAMHS professional and teacher in charge of the LSU.

The Pastoral Support Team meet weekly in a Pastoral Review Forum to report upon, advise and suggest interventions on issues that present as barriers to inclusion for identified students. This information is disseminated weekly via the Bulletin to all staff within the school. The data available to us at PRF provide an audit of the range of need within our school and ensure that the resources are effectively targeted at the areas of greatest need.

Monitoring

A termly multi-professional review and planning meeting is held with key personnel from the Behaviour Support Service, CAMHS, Brief Therapist, Educational Psychologist, SENCO, Refugee Co-ordinator, Lead Mentor and other agencies supporting inclusion within the school.

Termly monitoring meetings involve key personnel in school – for example, YCs, SENCO, the Educational Welfare Officer, assistant headteachers (AHTs), Inclusion Refugee Co-ordinator, Head of ethnic minority achievement – looking at issues affecting the achievement of particular groups of students within school including SEN students working below level 3 NC, refugees/asylum seekers, looked-after children, Roma students, students at risk of exclusion and students with physical/sensory disabilities supported through our Resource Base and other identified vulnerable students.

Attendance data is produced weekly, and our Strategic Management Group within the school considers behaviour data termly. The senior leadership team and the governors monitor the exclusion data on a termly basis.

Our overall inclusion policy can be determined by reference to our School Development Plan. This provides the evidence that a commitment to inclusion is owned and driven at the highest level within the school organisation. Our self-review of procedures and policies as well as our ongoing review of the School Development Plan provide a sound framework for supporting inclusion within South Camden Community School.

Our governing body actively supports, encourages and monitors our commitment to inclusive education through a programme of regular and ongoing reporting of key issues in the school, and our local education authority provides guidance and expertise and monitors the implementation of our combined school policies which support inclusion within the school.

Reviewed: June 2007   Date of next review: June 2009

Conclusion

Yes, it's a huge job. Nobody says you have to do it all yourself. The strategy and evaluation are definitely yours, but not necessarily alone. A lot of the rest will work better if you have a wide range of other people taking part of the role and feeling involved. You have governors, teachers, school leadership team, support and administrative staff, school improvement and advisory staff, parents, pupils and other agencies, as well as networks of Inclusion Managers in your local area. They can take on some of the responsibility, pass on ideas or act as a sounding board. Get them involved in your planning and diarise regular events, reviews and evaluation. And don't forget there is life beyond school and not everything needs doing in the first year!

Appendix

Example of an access plan

Reproduced with the kind permission of Rosemary Leeke, headteacher of South Camden Community School.

Access plan 2007–08

A disability is defined as a physical or mental impairment which has a substantial, long-term and adverse effect on a person's ability to carry out normal day-to-day activities.

The elements of the access plan cover the planning duty under the Disability Discrimination Act to plan for curriculum access, access to information, and physical and medical access.

The proposed actions are a result of ongoing planning and review following a Physical Access and Signage audit conducted in 2004/05 with the involvement of the LA. The plan also includes ongoing work arising from the access audit conducted with staff in 2003 that identified key areas for further development in ensuring curriculum access for identified students. These included:

Curriculum access

- Some ongoing training needed in supporting students working below National Curriculum Level 3.
- Lessons are not always responsive to pupil diversity.
- Planning time needed with additional support staff.
- School visits are not always accessible to all.
- Range of provisions needs to be developed to meet specific literacy, numeracy and EAL needs.
- Staff training requested in behaviour management strategies/student concerns about behaviour in lessons.

Access to information

- Review the provision of information to students, parents and carers who may have difficulty with standard printed forms.

Physical access

- Classrooms are not optimally organised for disabled students.
- Pathways and routes around school and parking arrangements are not well signed.
- Non-visual use of signs is not available.
- Some staff awareness is needed in technology and practices to assist people with
- Wheelchair-dependent students and/or staff could experience some barriers getting around school (corridors).

Medical access

- Ensure that procedures are in place to liaise with appropriate support agencies within the LA regarding students' medical/physical needs.
- Ensure that students have appropriate care plans that detail their specific physical and medical support needs.
- Ensure that staff receive the necessary training and support in relation to medical/physical needs of students.

This annual statement is backed up with several pages of planning under the headings Actions (e.g., Curriculum Access), Lead staff, Resources, Evidence of impact, Monitoring and Timeline.

Further reading

DCSF publications

DCSF/DfES publications can be found via the www.teachernet.gov.uk/publications website.
'Aiming High: Raising the achievement of Gypsy Traveller pupils' (2003), London.
'Aiming High: Understanding the educational needs of minority ethnic pupils in mainly white schools'
    (2004), London.
'Good Practice Guidance on the Education of Asylum Seeking and Refugee Children' (2003), London.
'School Supported Distance Learning', http://publications.teachernet.gov.uk/default.aspx?PageFunction=
    productdetails&PageMode=publications&ProductId=DFES-04073–2006& (2006), London.
'Special Educational Needs and Disability: Towards inclusive schools' (2004), London.
'Tracking for Success' (2005), London.

Ofsted publications

Ofsted publications can be found via the Publications and Research button on the www.ofsted.gov.uk
    site.
'The Education of Pupils with Medical Needs' (2003), London.
'Provision and Support for Traveller Pupils', www.ofsted.gov.uk/assets/3440.doc (2003).
'Using Data, Improving Schools' (2008), London.

QAA publication

'Designing a Personalised Curriculum for Alternative Provision' (2004), Gloucester.

Books

Cheminais, Rita. *Closing the Inclusion Gap: Special and mainstream schools working in partnership*. Taylor
    & Francis, 2003.
Hayward, Anne. *Making Inclusion Happen: A practical guide*. London: Paul Chapman Publishing, 2006.
Myers, Kate and Hazel Taylor, eds. *Genderwatch: Still watching*. Stoke-on-Trent: Trentham Books, 2006.
Saunders, Peter, ed. *Gypsies and Travellers in Their Own Words*. Leeds: Leeds Traveller Education Service,
    2000.
Tyler, Chris, ed. *Traveller Education: Accounts of good practice*. Stoke-on-Trent: Trentham Books, 2005.